WIDECOMBE-IN-THE-MOOR

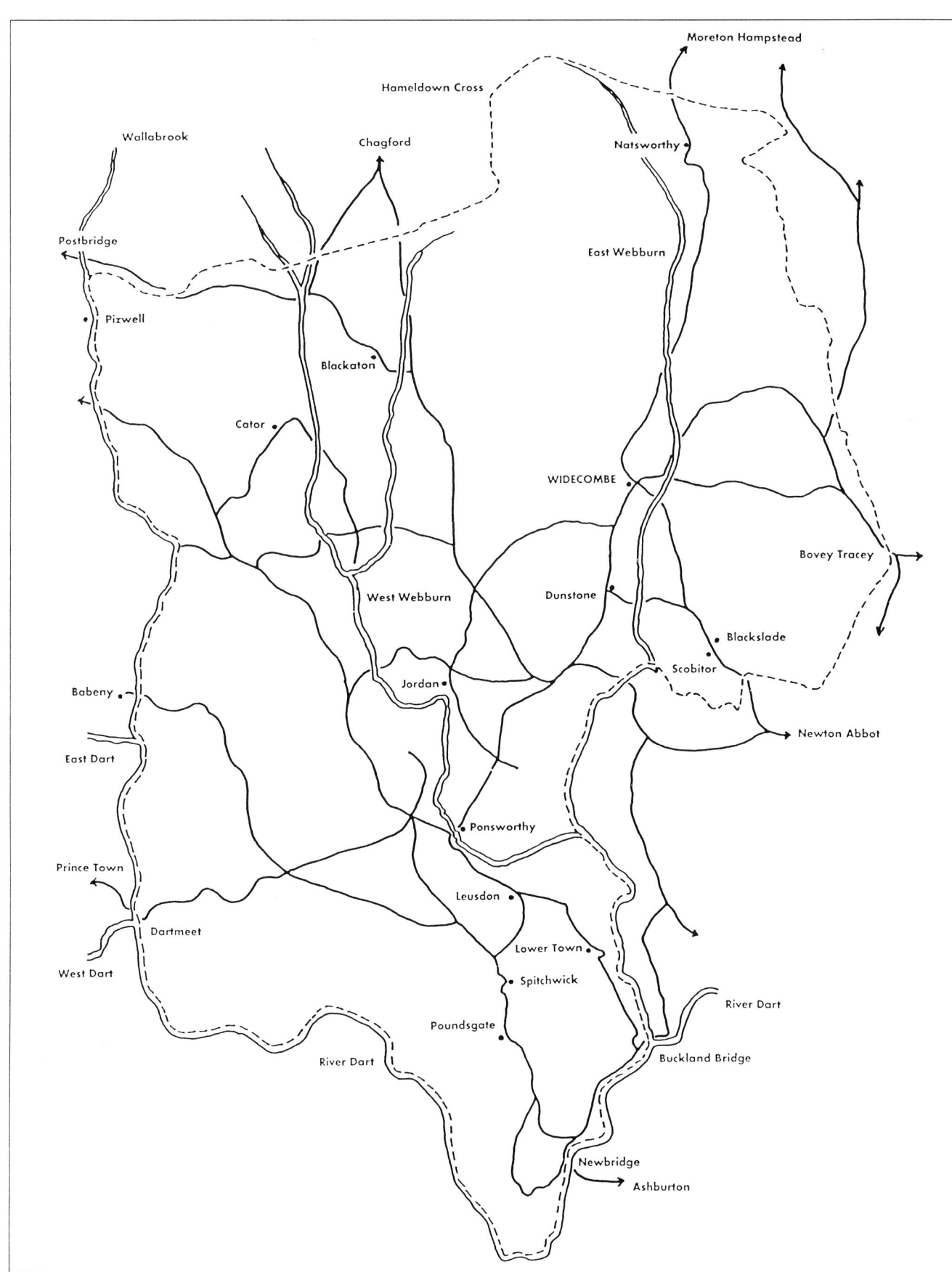

The Parish of Widecombe-in-the-Moor

WIDECOMBE-IN-THE-MOOR
A Pictorial History of the Dartmoor Village

Stephen H. Woods

DEVON BOOKS

First Published in 1996 by Devon Books

Copyright © 1996, Stephen H. Woods

All rights reserved. No part of this publication may be reproduced, stored in a retrieval system, or reproduced in any form or by any means without the prior permission of the copyright holder.

British Library Cataloguing in Publication Data

Catalogue Data for this book is available from the British Library

ISBN 0 86114 908 4

DEVON BOOKS
Official Publisher to Devon County Council

Halsgrove House
Lower Moor Way
Tiverton, Devon EX16 6SS
Tel: 01884 243242
Fax: 01884 243325

The photographs in this work are individually acknowledged and the copyright remains with the owner. If relevant, the origin of a picture is also stated. Where no source is given it may be taken that the photograph is from the author's collection or that the source is unknown.

The vignette on the title page is from a photograph taken at Brownberry c. 1900.

Printed and bound in Great Britain by Latimer Trend & Co. Ltd, Plymouth, UK.

DEDICATION

To all my family including the newest members Joel Christopher (23.10.96) and Anna Ellen (27.10.96).

But especially to Christopher who was so proud of his father's first book *Dartmoor Stone*, and who did not live to see its publication.

Widecombe-in-the-Moor: an aerial view of the centre of the village.

FOREWORD

The publication of this book will bring a great deal of pleasure to many people, not least all those who live in the parish of Widecombe-in-the-Moor or who have family connections there. It results from many years of work on the part of Stephen Woods who carried on the research originally undertaken by his mother. This is not an academic study but a simple record of parish life over the centuries. Indeed what is published here is but a fraction of the material the author has gleaned from old documents and about half the original number of photographs he collected. Alas, the costs of producing such a massive work in its entirety would put it beyond the pockets of all but a few and it has been a principle of its publication, that this book should be available to as many people as possible.

It is unusual for the publisher of a work also to contribute the foreword. In this instance I am happy to break this rule for Stephen is a friend and his first book *Dartmoor Stone* remains among the most satisfying of all the hundreds of books I have published over the years. This latest volume is an example of the best of local history publications for it springs from within the community it portrays and the author's passion for the place and its people shines through on every page.

As the world changes so communities such as that at Widecombe eventually change too, as the photographs here vividly remind us. How easily such images are lost as families move away from the district, as people die and as their effects are passed on or disappear. That box of old photographs, so precious to those who knew the faces of family and friends and who took part in the events captured by the camera, simply become a collection of old pictures in the hands of others. If for no other reason Stephen's work in obtaining and identifying such photographs is invaluable, for this book takes on the role of a permanent photo album and thus becomes an important historical document in itself.

It would be a marvellous thing to produce a similar work for every parish in the county. Regrettably there are too few people with Stephen's skill and dedication. Widecombe-in-the-Moor is fortunate to have him.

Simon Butler
Devon Books
November 1996

Iris Marion McCrea, the author's mother, c. 1915.

CONTENTS

Foreword	vii
Introduction	xi
The Prehistoric People	17
Robert Dymond - Antiquarian	22
Saxon and Norman Settlements	25
Ordinacio de Lideford AD 1260	35
The Manor Farms and Ancient Tenements	37
The Estate of Lano de Cadetrew	42
Dunstone Cottage	44
The Glebe Farm and Vicarage	46
The Cathedral of the Moor	49
The Church House	63
Other Places of Worship	65
The Churchwardens	69
Overseers of the Poor	71
Parish Schools	75
Tradesmen and Women	89
The Farmer and His Labourer	113
Transport	129
The Village Green	143
Widecombe Fair	145
Sporting Life and Leisure	149
For King and Country	153
Two Village Inns	154
Beating the Bounds	155
My Lady of the Moor	157
List of Subscribers	159

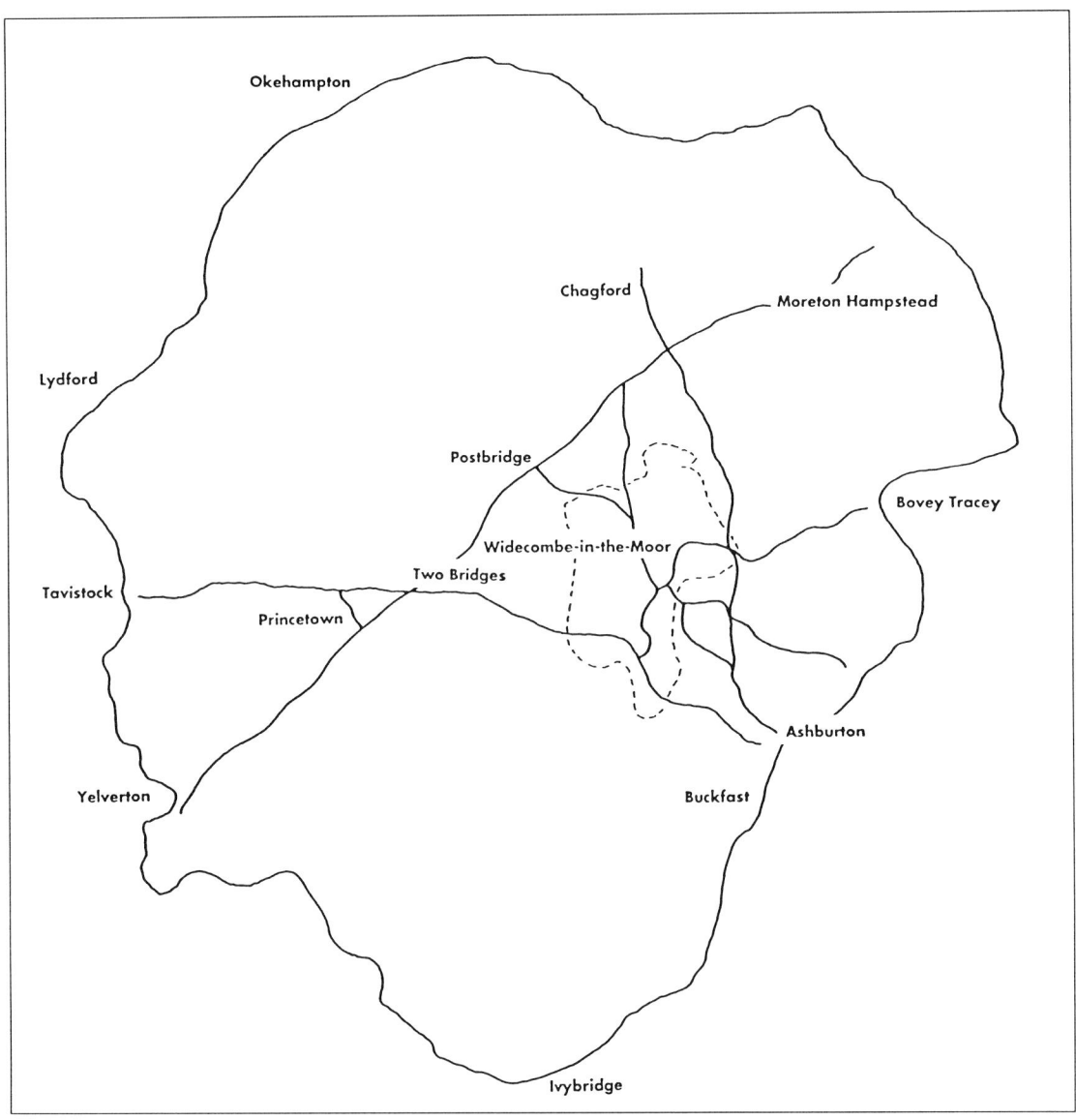

Dartmoor: a map showing the boundary of the Dartmoor National Park and the main roads. The borders of Widecombe parish are shown as a broken line.

INTRODUCTION

This book is written for my mother, Iris Woods (1897-1990), who came to Widecombe on holidays (as I do), with her family, the McCreas of Exeter. For the last thirty years of her life she lived in the parish and, spurred on by her enormous appetite for research, she sought to know the people among whom she lived.

This book should really be hers for I have her notes and writings. My own interest is photography, and Dartmoor. With my own meagre knowledge I have set down this history using only a small proportion of all the documentation that is available and which itself could fill several volumes.

It would seem appropriate to start a parish history by defining its boundaries but, as we shall see, the influence of Widecombe is cast far into the heart of the moor. Indeed, the parish and village is perhaps one of the best known in the whole of the country.

The area covered in this book incorporates three great ridges of Dartmoor intersected by the valleys of the East and West Webburn rivers. To the east is the ridge topped by the granite masses of Chinkwell Tor, Honeybag Tor, Bell Tor, Bonehill Rocks, Top Tor, Pil Tor and Tunhill Rocks. The central ridge, the great rolling hogsback of Hameldown, runs southwards to Wind Tor before dropping into the deep valley of the Dart at New Bridge. The south and western heights are crowned by Sharp, Yar, and Corndon Tors, though many other prominences beside these tors stand on the skyline of the parish. This is a rugged land populated by hardy people. In my book *Dartmoor Stone* I illustrated Dartmoor in its granite setting. This book concentrates on its people.

A few days after the publication and launch of *Dartmoor Stone*, on 9 December 1989, at the Church House Widecombe, I received a letter from my friend Freda Wilkinson containing these prophetic words: 'I found it a very moving occasion for many reasons, amongst all those friendly faces there were a lot of friendly ghosts: Edith and Hermon French, Ronnie Cave-Penny, Sam Cannon, Peter Hannaford, and of course, Christopher.'

I realised then how I had failed in my obligation to all those past writers who had stirred my emotions and who had encouraged me to discover more of this wonderful land. I considered how authors such as the Reverend and Mrs Bray, the Reverend Rowe, the Worths, Baring-Gould and William Crossing had not only recorded historical facts but had written down memories and traditions from the local people. I felt that I had neglected to take proper account of what the parishioners could tell me.

I was determined to discover more of what I came to call 'known history'. Winifred French kindly sent me the Southcombe diaries (1896, 1902, 1919, 1920 and 1922-31) which told much of the day-to-day life of the farmer and his labourer. Kit Hall lent me the Dymond diaries, beginning in 1870 and covering over a hundred years of that family's life.

Old photographs and ephemera flooded in: bills from shops that no longer existed; her father's rule book for the Rugglestone Inn Club, founded in 1836, sent to me by Deborah Hannaford. Such records of 'known history', reaching back over 150 years, bring to life the stories of the people who lived in the parish during that time. There is an added thrill when one's own family history leaps from the page as in the case of the entry in the Dymond diaries dated 10 August 1896: 'a short visit by Effie to the McCreas of Exeter who are staying at the buildings.' (Haytor). This is the year before my mother, Iris McCrea was born. Entries in the Southcombe diaries record: 'Miss McCrea was here' and 'Mr A. McCrea pd for potatoes 7/-' (this was my great-grandfather, one time Sheriff of Exeter).

Other entries speak of people and families known so well: 'G. Hambley and L.E. Kernick married.' (19 June 1924). George Hambley was in partnership with Percy Prouse, the last partnership to work at the old forge in Widecombe, and Lily Hambley, who played alongside my mother on the green, and who together hid their dolls in the roots of the giant sycamore, became secretary to Beatrice Chase for many years. She also played the organ in the church and at Dunstone chapel. It was she who provided me with the photographs of wheelbinding outside the forge.

A little glimpse of history is provided by entries such as that describing the 23rd Highland Regiment in full regalia, led by their band of pipes and drums, marching past the New Inn (Warren House Inn) at 4am on 24 August, 1873 on their way to join seven thousand men camped at Merripit Hill. Also entries: '6th March 1902 - HHH and JH and Matty to Widecombe to animated pictures;' '6th August 1920 - Car arrived'. Perhaps the first car ever to be owned in the parish.

Another invaluable source of information came from Ena Prowse (the ladies of that family spell their name with a 'w' and the men with a 'u') who wrote: 'Of course I remember you and your family, starting with your great grandparents. I was a very small child, about three I suppose, but I can remember how fascinated I was by your great granny's cute little bonnet tied under her chin with ribbons - and I wished my granny had one like it! Also her long black skirts and cape (the grandeur of which impressed me greatly). Her husband had a deep voice and a beard, and I was somewhat in awe of him.'

Ena added a postcript containing information I had not been looking for: 'I well remember those little sailor suits you wore to Chapel.'!

My research has thrown up a good few local 'worthies', many of whom appear throughout this book. Others, such as the Archbishop of Armagh, are names that appear fleetingly in ancient records and are otherwise lost. In 1347 he was a member of the Fitz Richard family of North Hall; nothing else about his Widecombe connections has come to light.

Another character was simply known as Lark. He lived rough around the parish at the turn of this century. He had no roof over his head but if anyone required a salmon, or half a dozen trout, a brace of pheasants, a couple of rabbits, or a hare, just to mention it to Lark was good enough. There they would be on your doorstep next morning.

Living rough in all weathers took its toll on Lark's clothes which got filthier and filthier. My great grandmother could not bear to see him in such a state and she turned to her husband and said 'You've got an old suit upstairs you don't wear. Give it to him.' Which he did.

Imagine her face when on the following day she saw Lark coming up the path, his face wreathed in smiles, proudly wearing his new suit over the top of his old clothes!

When Lark died he was buried in Widecombe churchyard in an unmarked grave alongside thousands of others who have contributed to our parish history.

A name recurring throughout this work is that of Hermon French. He was such a talented and knowledgeable man who told me about farming, showed me how to look for prehistoric flints, showed me a green patch in a ploughed field where two curlew eggs had been laid, while the mother bird walked in the adjacent furrow safe in knowing that here was a friend.

Though quiet and retiring, Hermon was also full of fun. He tried to teach me how to use a scythe but I either missed the grass altogether or drove the point into the ground. He took the scythe from me and moved up the field, the grass falling before him as he walked.

His family tree epitomises the difficulty in keeping track of the relationships which exist in a small community such a Widecombe. Thomas and Harriet French lived at Rowbrook in 1861 and had four children, Mary Jane, Emlyn, William and John Herbert. Thomas French was killed by a bull at Parklands, Spitchwick, in 1876.

Mary Jane married Richard French of Huccaby and later of Rowbrook. They had nine children, Richard Henry (who left home, fate unknown); Lavinia (married, burnt to death at the open fireplace at Rowbrook); Thomas (a Methodist preacher who married Jessie Langdon and lived at Rowden - Hermon French was their son); Thirza (unmarried, died at Rowbrook); Laura (married Henry Caunter of Ollsbrim); James (unmarried, died at Rowbrook); William (killed at Rowbrook); Frederick (married) and Harriet (lived at Dunnabridge).

The story of William's life is most extraordinary. His father was out working in the fields one day while a thunderstorm raged overhead and, looking up, he saw a streak of lightning strike the farm. Hurrying home he found that William had been killed as he lay in bed between two brothers, neither of whom had been touched.

Thomas and Harriet French's youngest son, John Herbert, married Thirza Chaffe and they went to live at Spitchwick and later at Corringdon. They had six children, Herbert John, Edith Elizabeth, Hermon, Nancy, Betty and Jasper (the latter who lived at Drywells, Wooder, and also later at Southcombe). I knew him well.

Edith Elizabeth married John Hannaford of Southcombe, and when John died she married her younger cousin Hermon, living at Dockwell where I spent many happy days in their company. After Edith died Hermon married Winifred. She once wrote to me saying 'Edith's father's sister was Hermon's father's mother' (i.e. Hermon's grandmother). She further confused matters by marrying a Mr French of Rowbrook! The people of Widecombe take delight in compounding such genealagical problems.

In researching for this book I have delved deeply into the two chests of parish documents. The parish chest was kept in the Church House, the other in the vestry - the latter holding the church documents which have now been transferred to the Devon Record Office.

The parishioners have a strong regard for their history and in the 1960s they took part in two surveys. In the first they recorded all field names in the parish; in the second they made a survey of the gravestones and monuments in the churchyard. Copies of both surveys were deposited in the parish chest.

I had a vision of old ladies lying on the gravestones armed with large sheets of paper and

INTRODUCTION

wax crayons! Phyllis Pascoe recently told me off for committing the same offence some twenty-five years later.

Thus my researches have taken me from the study of ancient records, to walks through the landscape, to stories told to me and to my mother by the people of Widecombe.

In writing this history I have to acknowledge the help given to me by the parishioners and those knowledgeable in parish affairs, especially Anthony Beard; Bessie Beard (deceased); Gwen Beard (deceased); Sidney Beard (deceased) for his personal recollections passed to me by his son Tony; Mark Beeson; Dave and Kath Brewer (for a host of information and for remembering to pass on information which came their way); Anstice Brown (for the loan of her mother's notes and a copy of the Dunstone and Blackslade Manor Courts); Arthur Brown (deceased); Jack Brown (deceased); Sam Cannon (deceased); Veronica Cave-Penny (deceased); Gordon Dawe; Audrey Erskine; Ted Fitch; Andrew Fleming; Bessie French; Hermon French (deceased); Winifred French (for files of notes collected by Hermon, and for the Southcombe Diares); Elizabeth Gawne (deceased); Jean Gooch; John Gooch (deceased); Tom Greeves; Elisabeth Greeves (née Stanbrook); Debbie Griffths; Kit Hall (for allowing access to the Dymond Diaries); Bob Hayes; Joan Hambleton; Lily Hambley (deceased); May Hambley (deceased); Marianne Margaret Hamlyn (deceased); Deborah Hannaford; Bob Haynes (deceased); William Hess; Molly Hill; Wilfred Jones; Katherine Longley (for translations); Gladys and Sylvester Mann; The Moorland Team Ministry; the Revd Brown; the Revd Bulley (deceased); the Revd Pearce Pound; Bill Saxon; Barbara Norrish; Michael Nosworthy; Thirza Nosworthy (deceased); Phyllis Pascoe; Margaret Price; Jack Prouse (for a cascade of letters full of personal recollections of Widecombe); Ena Prowse; Oliver Rackman; George Radford; Lady Sylvia Sayer; Jack Simpson; John Somers Cocks (for sending his own notes and transcriptions); Mary Stanbrook; Margaret Steemson; John Stone (deceased); Roger Thorne (for information on the Methodists); Raymond Warren (deceased); Violet Warren; Colin and Margaret Westwood; Marjorie and Geoff Weymouth; Freda Wilkinson; my father Albert Woods (deceased); my mother Iris Woods, née McCrea (deceased); my brother John Woods (deceased) and Rollo Woods.

I also gratefully acknowledge the assistance given by the following: The Duchy of Cornwall Office; Dartington Rural Archive; Institute of Agricultural History; Widecombe Parish Council (of which Lily Hambley was secretary for thirty-two years between 1942 and 1974). Thanks also for the gracious permission given by HRH Prince Charles, Duke of Cornwall, to quote from DCO London Dartmoor Proceedings 1786-1788, folio 90-95.

It should be noted that the full name of Widecombe-in-the-Moor is used locally and is maintained as something of a matter of local pride. In this book the name appears in both its full version and its shorter form of Widecombe, referring variously to the the central village ('Widecombe Town') and to the parish as a whole. Place names and personal names vary enormously where they appear in historical records and these differences have been retained in this work, otherwise the 'modern' form is generally used.

Tony Beard, in one of his many letters to me, wrote: 'I often feel that an author should be brave enough to state that which, to the best of his or her belief, is accurate, but to invite comments, variations on the detail, theories or further information, photos documents, etc. with the intention of updating the book sometime in the future, or better still producing another volume containing the fresh information...' I concur with this statement and would like to receive all such comments and information, or criticism, concerning this work.

Stephen H. Woods
Portchester
Hants PO16 8JP

Widecombe in the Moor c. 1900. *(Grant Norsworthy and Michael Nosworthy)*.

New Bridge, over the River Dart on the southern boundary of the parish. From a postcard by F. Frith & Co. Ltd c. 1910. *(Iris Woods collection)*.

INTRODUCTION

The road around Bonehill Rocks, with Bell Tor and Chinkwell Tor on the right and Hameldown in the distance. From a postcard c. 1920 by E.A. Sweetman & Son. *(Iris Woods collection).*

Ollsbrim Cross with Sharp Tor behind. This is one of the many wayside granite crosses of the moor. It once did service as a gatepost at Town Farm, Leusdon, and both its arms have been broken.

Above left: the old village sign was taken down in 1939 and was eventually replaced by the new sign (**right**) designed by Lady Sylvia Sayer. *(Iris Woods Collection).*

xv

WIDECOMBE

Above: Edith Elizabeth, Nancy and Betty: three daughters of John Herbert and Thirza French, Christmas 1916. *(Hermon French collection)*.

Left: Andrew McCrea, the author's great-grandfather, dressed in his ceremonial robes as Sheriff of Exeter. *(Iris Woods collection)*.

Above left: Anna McCrea (née Tucker), the author's great-grandmother, with her daughter Hilda McCrea, on a day out on Dartmoor c. 1910. *(Iris Woods collection)*.

Above and left: pages from a folio of drawings titled 'Hannaford 1888'. *(George Radford)*.

xvi

THE PREHISTORIC PEOPLE

The first people known to have visited the moorland waste of Dartmoor, later to include the parish of Widecombe, were the nomadic tribal groups whose name is taken from the tiny flint objects they left behind. These Mesolithic people used such tools as battered back knives and wedge-shaped arrowheads, which today can be found scattered about the parish - with good examples being found at Runnage and Dockwell.

Hermon French discovered a number of such flints protruding at the intersection of the growan (decomposed granite) and the peat layer in a small quarry made by road menders on the edge of the moor, east of Watergate. Unfortunately road workers now dump their surplus material on the same spot.

The Mesolithic age spanned the period 8000–4000 BC and it was during this time that men and women first established settlements, probably temporary, in the Widecombe area. These people were followed by the Neolithic tribes 4000–2500 BC, also nomadic, and who also left stone tools behind as evidence of their occupation. These include stone axes and distinctive leaf-shaped arrowheads. These people also left monuments such as stone rows, and chambered tombs.

Direct evidence for their occupation of Widecombe comes from a possible Neolithic tomb site, a mound on the lower flank of Hameldown, west of Natsworthy, and also from a field name on Chittleford Farm, Shelson Ley, a possible reference to a 'shelf stone' or capping stone of a Neolithic chamber.

The Bronze Age followed in the period 2500–600 BC and with it a more settled population. They left vast quantities of stone and metal weapons: barbed flint arrowheads, flint axes, bronze axes and daggers. Little of the metalwork has survived in Dartmoor's acidic soil although some examples have been discovered.

On Hameldown there are a group of seven barrows, three of which have a diameter greater than sixty feet, and include Broad Burrow, Single Burrow, Two Burrows and Hamilton (Hameldown) Beacon. These are believed to date c. 1550 BC.

Spence Bate, an archaeologist ahead of his time in investigative practice, methodically explored some of these barrows. In 1872, while excavating the northernmost of the Two Burrows, he came across five slabs lying on the surface of the subsoil, under which he unearthed the remains of a cremation with which was interred a bronze dagger blade and an amber pommel studded with gold.

This unique find was deposited in the museum in Plymouth where it was destroyed during the blitz in 1941.

However, photographs of the dagger blade and pommel survive and the *Antiquaries Journal* of 1937 provides the following description: 'It [the pommel] was cut from a single block of dark transparent amber of a warm reddish brown with a tawny gleam when held up to the light... the pointille ornament was made by drilling tiny holes about 2mm deep into the amber and tapping down into them a short length of gold wire which was then cut off flush with the surface. On the top of the pommel the decoration takes the form of a cruciform arrangement of two narrow triple rows of gold dots, a similar band runs round the lip.'

Throughout the Widecombe area the commonest finds are flint flakes, and the burin - the central core of flint from which flakes were knocked before being shaped into tools. Such finds are difficult to date, as are scrapers and spindle whorls.

However, the Bronze Age people left clearer evidence of their occupation, a host of buildings and monuments, the remain of many of which can be seen today: hut circles, enclosures, cists, cairns, barrows, stone rows and circles.

About 1600 BC two large Bronze Age communities overlaid the parish: one covered the area of Rippon Tor, crossing over what is now the parish boundary to descend into the Widecombe Valley rising up on to the flank of Hameldown. The other community spread from the edge of Holne Moor, across the river Dart and over Vaghill, Yar Tor and Corndon Down. These people divided their land by constructing stone and earth barriers known as reaves, pronounced locally as 'raves'. They then subdivided the land by a series of parallel reaves and it becomes obvious from ground evidence, from maps and aerial photography, that the historic farmer utilised these walls to form the fields of their farms.

Evidence from hut circles excavated at Foales Arrishes show that habitation continued into the Iron Age (600 BC–AD 43).

Though they left no written record, such evidence as remains in abundance on the Dartmoor landscape, provides a vivid picture of these early farming communities.

Towards the end of the Bronze Age the climate changed and drove these people from the high lands of Dartmoor.

WIDECOMBE

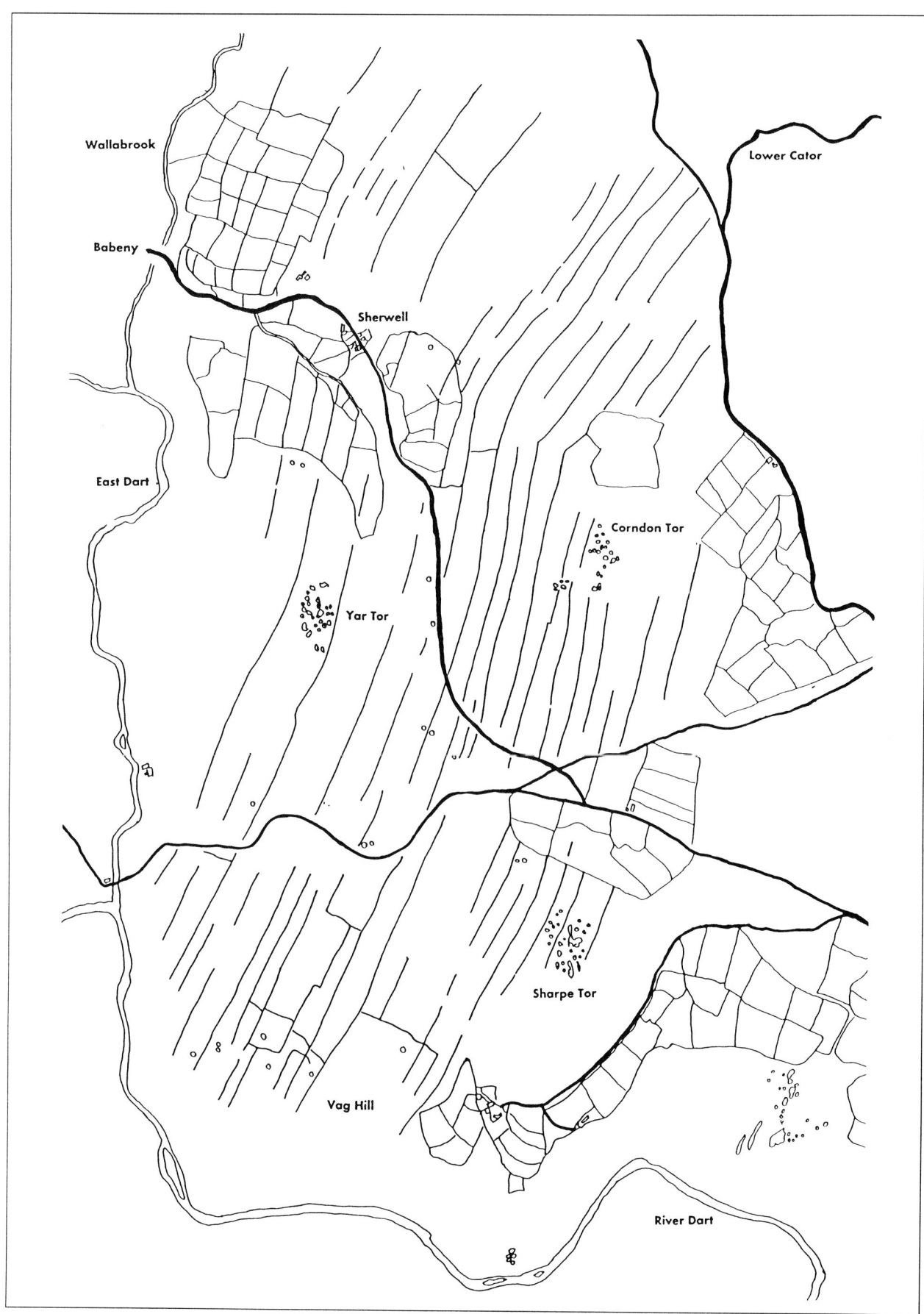

Part of the Bronze Age reave system in Widecombe parish

THE PREHISTORIC PEOPLE

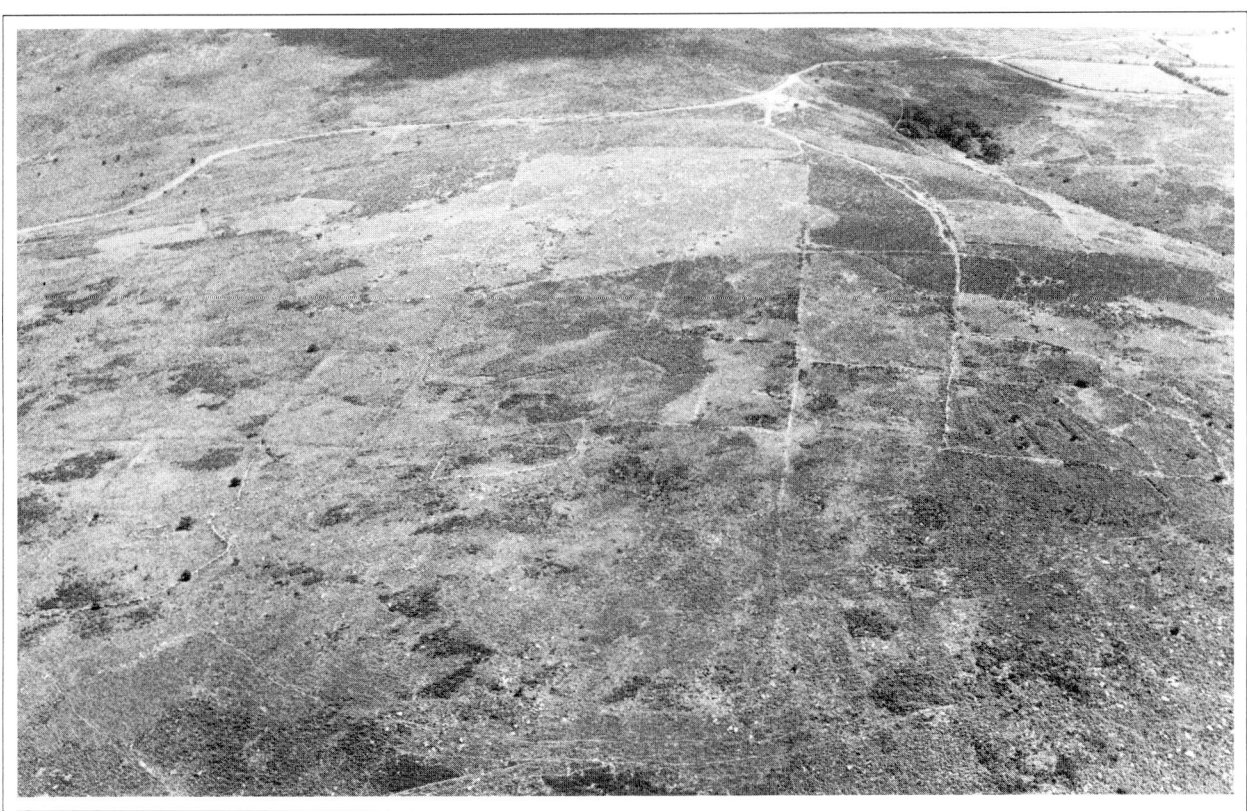

This aerial photograph reveals the parallel lines of the reave system on Vaghill Warren.

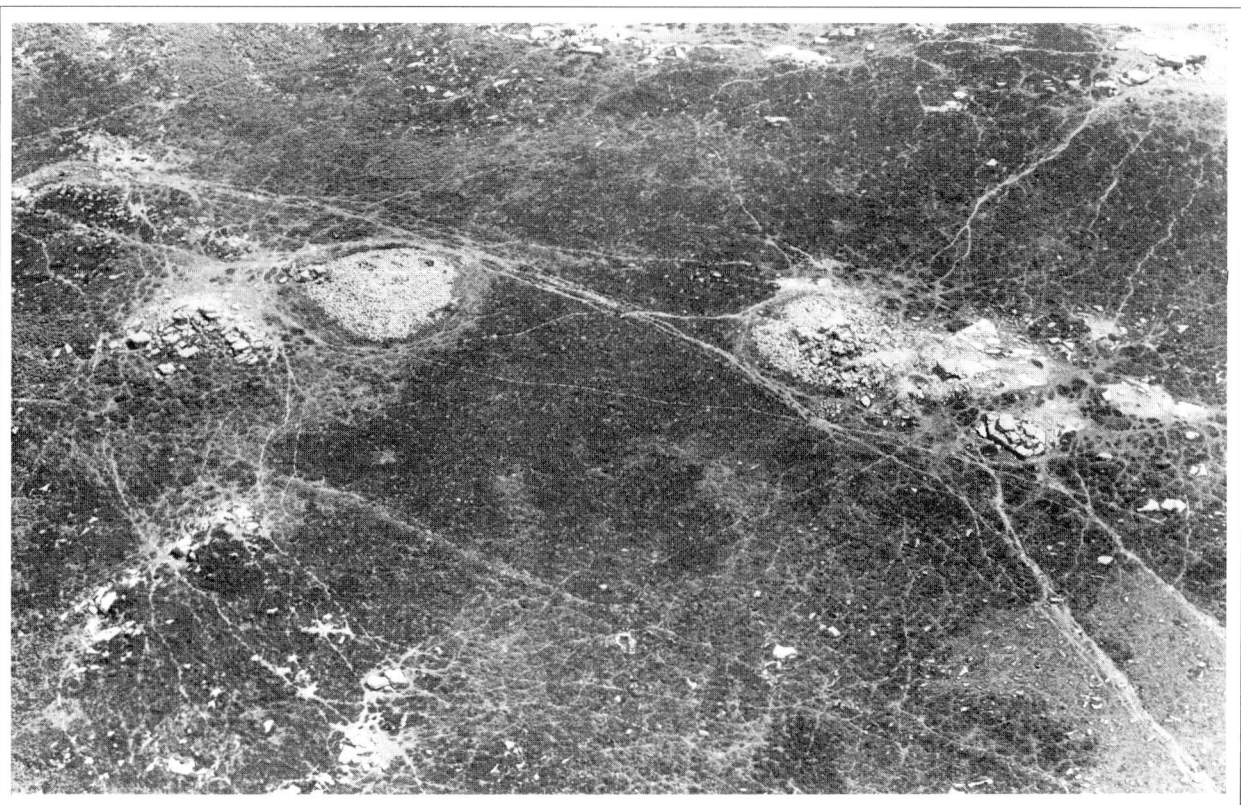

Two prehistoric cairns lie against the tors on the summit of Corndon Tor.

WIDECOMBE

Above: Mesolithic battered back knives. *(Hermon French collection).*

Above: Neolithic stone axe found at Huccaby. *(Hermon French collection).*

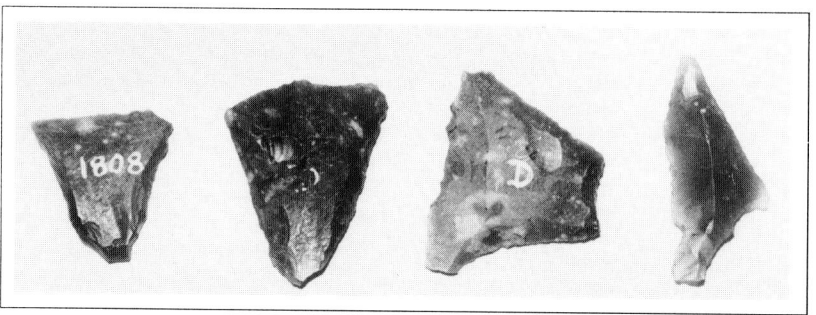

Left: Mesolithic chisel arrowheads. *(Hermon French collection).*

Above: Neolithic leaf-shaped arrowheads. *(Hermon French Collection).*

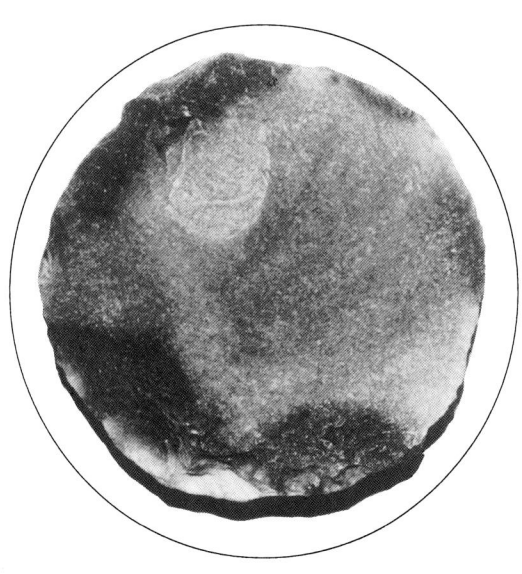

Above: Bronze Age flint axehead, found by Tom Nosworthy at Shallowford. *(Thirza Nosworthy)*

Left: flint scraper found at Poundsgate *(courtesy: John Woods).*

THE PREHISTORIC PEOPLE

Right: Bronze Age axehead found at Corringdon Farm, South Brent and a whetstone found on Riddon ridge. Note how perfectly the axehead fits the shape of the whetstone. *(Hermon French collection).*

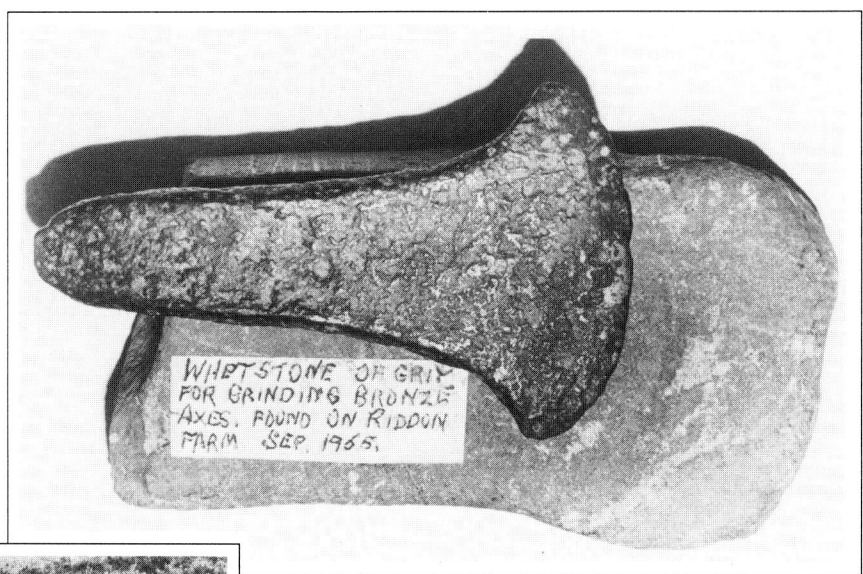

Below: a cist (burial chamber) on Hameldown, near Stoneslade Tor.

Above: a tall stone, of menhir proportions, ends a stone row under Laughter Tor. The sheepstell wall can be seen on the left.

Above left: stone row, circle and cist on Lakehead Hill.

Left: cist and cairn circle on the edge of Soussons plantation. Recorded as 'Ringaston' in the Perambulation of Spitchwick Manor.

ROBERT DYMOND - ANTIQUARIAN

A great benefactor of Widecombe, Robert Dymond was born on 8 September 1821; dying at Blackslade on Friday 31 August 1888, surrounded by his family. What aroused his interest in Dartmoor, and Widecombe in particular, is uncertain, for his first love was writing. He was a member of Exeter's Literary Society for many years.

His father was also called Robert, an estate agent, and he and his son carried out business together with younger brother, Frank, whose devotion to duty was to see him undertake an epic journey following the Great Blizzard of 1891.

It was probably through business connections that Robert junior came to buy Dunstone Manor, residing at Blackslade from 1869. Here he brought his wife Josephine (née Hingston) whom he married in 1851, and their three children, Arthur Hingston Dymond, Caroline (Carrie), and Josephine (Effie).

Carrie was to marry Louis H. Tosswill, and she bore him eight children, although the first born, Bertram, his grandfather's pride and joy, died before the others were born.

Effie never married. She became a respected deaconess and, on her mother's death in 1913, Effie became Lady of the Manor. Since then Dunstone and Blackslade Manor have continued with a succession of Ladies: Olive Awdry and Anstice Brown.

Robert Dymond became a respected member of Exeter's community, a member of the Harleian Society, a committe member of the Royal Albert Memorial Museum and a dedicated member of the Devonshire Association to which he contributed many papers. He was a leading light of the Teign Naturalists Field Club - seventy members of which once met on the green in Widecombe where Dymond addressed them before taking them to tea at Blackslade. In 1872 he was appointed a magistrate and was also admitted as a Fellow of the Society of Antiquaries.

But, for this author, above all he will be remembered and honoured for his involvement with the people of Widecombe; not just as Lord of the Manor of Dunstone, but for his strenuous efforts to protect and restore the church of St Pancras, centre of parish life.

In 1876 he edited and largely wrote a book *Things New and Old Concerning the Parish of Widecombe-in-the-Moor*. This he did to raise money to restore the church which he felt was falling down around his head, being neglected for many years.

He also inspired his family to record their personal involvement with the moor in a series of family diaires which have been updated and continued within the family for over a century.

It is likely that both Robert and his wife had connections with the Society of Friends, being referred to in the diaries as 'The Father' and 'The Mother'.

Recording day-to-day events in family life, the diaries also provide an insight into early archaeological investigations of Dartmoor: Spence Bate's work at Two Barrows and Grimspound, and Robert Burnard's work at Foales Arrishes.

A drawing from the Dymond diaries of Blackslade, following renovations there in 1876.

ROBERT DYMOND - ANTIQUARIAN

The Tosswill family outside Blackslade: **standing** (l-r) Rose Marion - later Mrs J.P. Hepburn; Mabel Josephine; Maurice Julian - became a Torquay solicitor; Leonard Robert - became of doctor in London; **seated** (l-r) Louis Henry FRCS - an oculist in Exeter; Anstice Evelyn - later Mrs F.E. Hall, wife of Canon Hall of Leusdon; Bernard Hingston - emigrated to New Zealand; Olive Muriel - later Mrs R.W. Awdry; Caroline Anne - wife of Dr L.H. Tosswill.

Robert Dymond bought Dunstone and Blackslade Manor from William Norrish, and bequeathed it to Deaconess Josephine 'Effie' Dymond of Ashburton. She in turn left it to Olive Muriel Awdry in 1930, who gave it to her daughter Mrs Anstice Brown in 1961. Mrs Brown wrote to the author in 1991 'I have given it to my son, Richard John Brown'.

Above: Josephine 'Effie' Dymond. **Right:** 'The Mother' Josephine Dymond (née Hingston) and 'The Father', Robert Dymond. *(Anstice Brown).*

WIDECOMBE

Hutholes, the remains of a pre-Conquest settlement at Dockwell. It comprises six buildings, including two dwellings built on the traditional longhouse pattern. This is one of several deserted farm sites in the parish.

SAXON AND NORMAN SETTLEMENTS

The first people to leave written evidence were the immigrant Saxons who fought, colonised and put down their roots - although in Widecombe there is no evidence that they deposed anyone from existing dwellings.

We have three documents only pertaining to this period: the first is a grant by King Eadwig in AD 957; the second a working copy of the bounds set out in the Peadington[tun] Charter of 1050; and the third, and later document, the Domesday Book.

The 'Grant by King Eadwig to the Lady Aethelhild of lands at Ipplepen, Abbots Kerswell, etc.' is probably an inaccurate thirteenth-century copy which sets out the bounds of the lands concerned but concludes: 'Jaet Bitelanwysthe an hiwisce. Jaet Bromleage an hiwisce.' This can possibly be translated as 'and [in addition to the lands whose boundaries are already given, I grant] one hide at Bittleford, and one hide at Brimley.' Bittleford is therefore the first recorded placename in Widecombe - and still exists today - though it was not recorded in Domesday.

What has become known as the Peadington Charter is that part of an original document setting out the bounds of a land grant. Only the first four lines of that document are relevant here for they detail that part of the boundary that crosses Widecombe parish.

It starts:

> 'Pis is Peading tunes landscaro paer œscburne ut scyt'
> On dertan (st) ream od pede burne ut scyt.
> up an pede burnan op pidi mor.
> Of pidi more on cealfa dune middepearde.'

Katherine Longley translated this as: 'This is the boundary of the country of the people of Padda there: from all the œscburne outfall along the Dert stream up to the Wedeburne outfall, along the Wedeburne as far as Withimoor, from Withimore to Caelfadune.'

The Saxon meaning of Wedeburne, now the Webburn, is 'raging stream' - and evidence of this ferocity was given in the great storm of 1938 (see page 134).

The problem for those who study this document is that at Lizwell Meet the Webburn divides into its East and West branches (the East Webburn was in 1526 referred to as the Neperell). If the boundary followed the West Webburn it is also interesting to note that it followed the boundary line between the manors of Spitchwick and Jordan. This route would take it over Challacombe (Cealfadune?) Down.

Davidson, who brought the document to light, interpreted the boundary as going up the East Webburn to Dunstone Down and then over Hameldown. Whatever the merits of these discussions on the course of the boundary, the document provides some food for thought concerning the origins of the placename of Widecombe.

The present author's family cottage at Dunstone was taken in from fields known as Willow Piece and Second Willow Piece (there were also Third and Fourth Willow Pieces) which stretched up the side of Dunstone Down. A document of 1750 refers to these fields as 'Willagieres': as shrub is to shrubbery, so willow is to willagery. The Old English name for willow is *Welige*, commonly a withy - which leads us to Withycombe and, through time, to Widecombe.

There are numerous variations on the spelling of this name throughout history: Withecombe, Widdicum, Widecomb, Widdicombe; and in coinage duty records: Wythicombe, Wethycombe and Wethecomb.

The Great Domesday Book, the Exchequer version, is an abridged compilation of a number of other Domesday recordings. We are fortunate that the Exeter (Exon) Domesday, covering the South West, survives in the Exeter Cathedral library, for it records more detail than the Exchequer version.

The Domesday record is not a census for it ignores women and children, among others. It does however record the names of those who owned the land in 1086, its chief tenant, and the previous pre-Conquest landlord who owned it in 1066 T.R.E. (that is, the day that King Edward was both alive and dead).

The smallest division recorded is the manor or estate, and in Widecombe there are six certain references to holdings known today as: 1. Spitchwick, 2. Natsworthy, 3. Dunstone, 4. Blackslade, 5. Scobitor, 6. Jordan. No reference is made to Widecombe itself which clearly did not exist at that time.

It is possible that the site of the church of St Pancras was chosen as being convenient to the manors of Natsworthy, Blackslade and Dunstone, standing as it does on the 'Saxon' road between Dunstone and Natsworthy, probably at a junction where another road ran to Blackslade and Scobitor - also on a direct route to Jordan (Hutholes).

It is likely at this time that land was cleared for North Hall which is closely associated with Widecombe Town Manor.

HUTHOLES

The strongest evidence of settlement in the Saxon period at Widecombe lies in the form of the visible ruins of long-abandoned dwellings. These people built their settlements: manor house, farmstead, cottage and barn, as a small compact unit, usually at the edge of the treeline. As the land was gradually cleared, other farms were established, for instance at Chittleford and Venton, below Blackslade.

A more definite pattern can be seen below Natsworthy, with numerous farms being created in what were possibly woodland clearings, referred to in Domesday as 'coppice' (an area of wood being cropped). At the foot of the valley lay 'Wooda' (Wooder today).

Of the several deserted settlement sites in the parish, Hutholes revealed some interesting evidence during excavations carried out by E. Marie Minter in the 1960s. The site lies on Dockwell Farm in an enclosure below Rowden Ball in the manor of Jordan. The remains showed six buildings, including two traditional longhouses and a corn drying barn. Excavations showed many rebuildings had taken place of turf houses supported by timber, the earliest dating from around AD 800.

The site, like many others on Dartmoor, was abandoned in the thirteenth or fourteenth century at a time when the climate deteriorated and the Black Death ravaged the population.

An earlier name for Hutholes might be South Rowden. In 1719 William Bogan had to mortgage his land in the area and among these he lists 'two messuages or tenements called North Rowdons' one of 17 acres, the other of 19 acres, in the possession of John Hannaford, or under his tenants. Another messuage, called South Rowden, estimated to be 37 acres, was in the hands of John Hamlin or his undertenants, plus commons known as Rockwill, containing 60 acres, 'to the said several tenements called North Rowdons adjoining or belonging'.

The mortgage contains the contingency 'be it more or less' thus making it impossible to precisely define the lands in question, but the proximity of South Rowdon to Hutholes makes it likely that these are the same place.

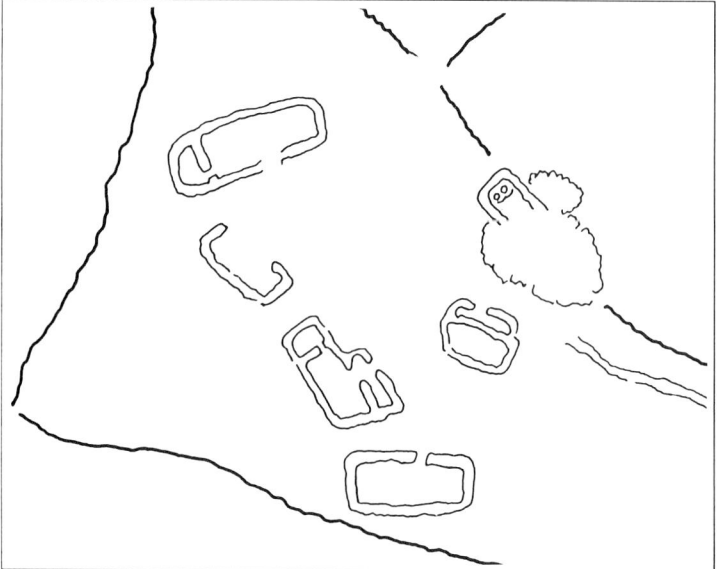

The settlement at Hutholes follows a pattern typical of such sites on Dartmoor, small dwellings clustered among associated farm buildings and field walls. The aerial photograph on page 24 reveals the compact nature of the settlement.

Left: a plan of the site. **Below left:** the two-roomed longhouse (shown at the top of the plan). **Below right:** a 'cache' found in the three-roomed longhouse (centre of the plan), possibly the Saxon manor house *Depdona* (Deptone).

SAXON AND NORMAN SETTLEMENTS

MANOR OF SPITCHWICK

'The king has a manor called ESPICEWITA (Exch. SPICEWITA) which Earl Harold held T.R.E. and it paid geld for 1 hide. This 8 ploughs can till. Thereof the king has half a hide in demense and the villeins half hide and 4 ploughs. There the king has 8 villeins, 4 bordars, 5 serfs, wood(land) 1 league length by 1 furlong in breadth and 100 acres of pasture. It pays 60 shillings by weight, when Baldwin received it the same.' - Domesday Book.

This extract is from the Exeter Domesday Book, published in the *Victoria County History*. The Exchequer Domesday Book omits the fact that 'the king held half in demesne' and that its value was the same when Baldwin took possession.

The Manor of Spitchwick has changed hands very infrequently. Dr Thomas Blackall bought it from the descendants of Lord Ashburton in 1869; Mr Struben was the purchaser in 1902, and Jack Simpson's father became Lord of the Manor in 1934. The manor remains in the hands of the Simpson family who see the importance of maintaining the ancient manorial traditions. When the Jury and Homage meet today, the Commoners still appoint their Reeve, Tythingman, Aletaster and Poundkeeper.

The records of the manor from 1714-1747 and 1752 are held at the Devon Record Office. Since 1786 the records have been kept in a beautifully bound leather book entitled *Manor of Spitchweeke*.

This volume records the names of the jurors who were sworn in at the Court Leet held at the house of John Townsend at Poundsgate in 1786. These were: Peter Hamlyn, John Arnell, John Hext, Richard Hext, Henry Caunter, Walter Windeat, Henry Stockman, Walter Windeat jnr, Sylvester Mann, Robert Mead, Thomas Hamlyn Sherwill and James Townsend

The current Lord of the Manor, Jack Simpson, has produced a replica volume which records the Jury and Homage for 1980, when the Commoners chose Mr J. Wilkinson as Foreman, John Irish as Reeve, Simon Partridge as Tythingman and Aletaster, and Alec Turner as Poundkeeper.

Another treasured possession is a map of the manor on which is recorded the comments of those who have perambulated the bounds in 1869, 1898, 1902, 1924 and 1937. As most of the manor boundary follows the course of the rivers Dart, Wallabrook and Webburn, it is not surprising to find a number of the beaters got their feet wet. They had a tradition of claiming the islands in the river as being in the manor, either by walking round them or by breaking off some of the undergrowth.

The map shows that a track from Lower Town to Buckland Church, known as 'Lady's Path', crossed the Webburn by stepping stones or a 'clam' (stone bridge), erected fifty years before the 1869 perambulation by Lady Ashburton. The bridge across the Wallabrook at Riddon was built by Peter Mann sixty years before the same perambulation.

The distance around the manor is approximately sixteen miles of hard going. At the last two perambulations Jack Simpson has given all those who finish a commemorative china mug bearing the words 'Spitchwick Perambulation' and giving the date.

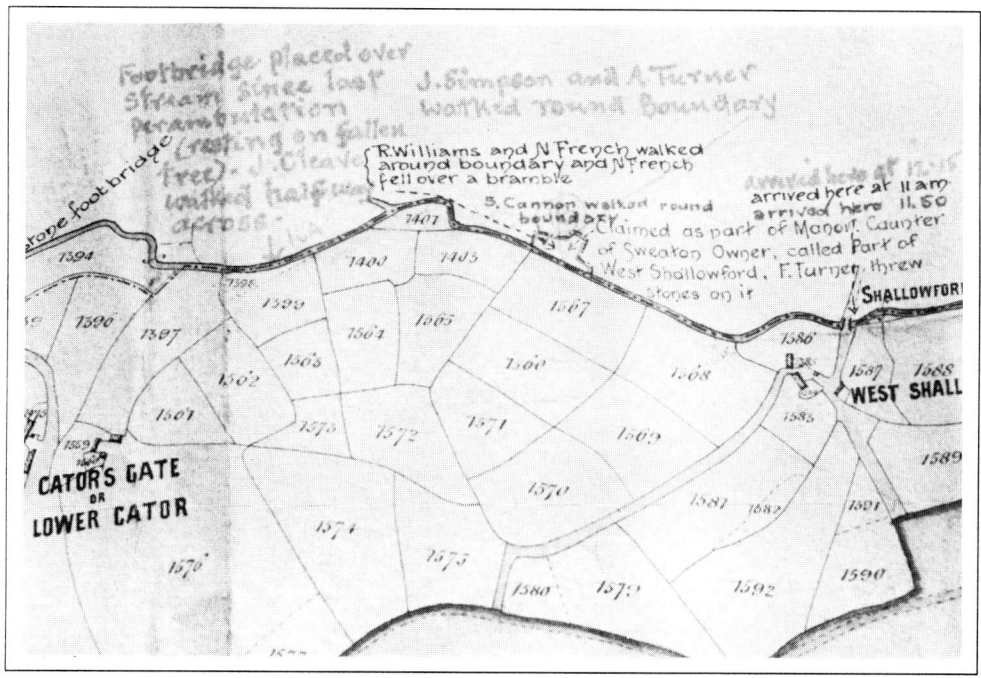

A section of the Spitchwick Manor map showing some of the notes appended by those beating the bounds.
Such perambulations of parish or manor boundaries were an important function in past times in order to establish the exact extent of ownership or responsibility.

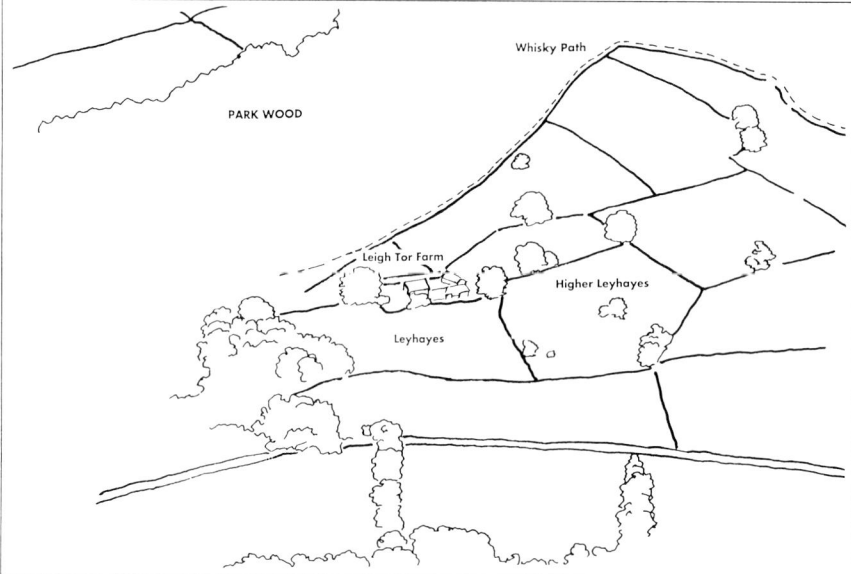

Park Wood and Leigh Tor Farm. The photograph shows part of Park Wood with the possible ditch and wall of the park running along what is now known as Whisky Path.

The wood at Spitchwick recorded in Domesday matches the dimensions of Park Wood, shown in the photograph and plan above. The name 'Park' provokes thoughts of a deer park here. Certainly the king loved to hunt and he retained half of Spitchwick for himself.

Saxon and Norman deer parks are rare; they were constructed for the maintenance and protection of deer herds, mainly fallow deer. Each park would have a ditch and a substantial fence or wall around its perimeter. Evidence of such a wall and ditch exists on the south side of Park Wood, the ditch today forming a track known locally as Whisky Path.

The Normans also hunted wild pigs and one possible derivation of the place name of Spitchwick is 'Wic', being farm, and 'Spic' being bacon.

A document believed to date from before 1290 is a 'Charter of feoffment, William, Lord of Spickwyk to Hamelin Carpenter'. It describes an area of land in the manor 'together with common pasture with all animals in the waste land between Throubrok and Haneworth, and also in the wasteland on the west side of Leghtorre, especially with pigs, goats etc.'

Throubrok is likely to be today's Rowbrook and Haneworthy is probably derived from 'Hannas Worthy', now Hannaford, ancient home of that family.

SAXON AND NORMAN SETTLEMENTS

NATSWORTHY

'Richard (son of Turold) himself holds NOTESWRDE. Edward held it T.R.E. and it paid geld for 1 ferling. Arable for 2 ploughs which are there with 1 serf, 2 villeins, and 2 bordars. Five acres of meadow are there and 6 acres of coppice. Formerly worth 5 shillings, now worth 15 shillings.' - Domesday Book

It seems likely that the original manor was close to the present farms and cottages of Middle and Lower Natsworthy, rather than the more modern Natsworthy Manor. The aerial photograph shows the hamlet lying at one end of a series of medieval stripfields stretching to Hedge Barton, with an access road along one side.

The '6 acres of coppice' suggests an industry for a growing population, coppice being underwood trees which are cut down to a stump, known as a stool, every few years. From the stool, tall straight shoots grow which can be harvested periodically. An oak, for instance, might grow an inch-thick shoot seven feet tall in one season.

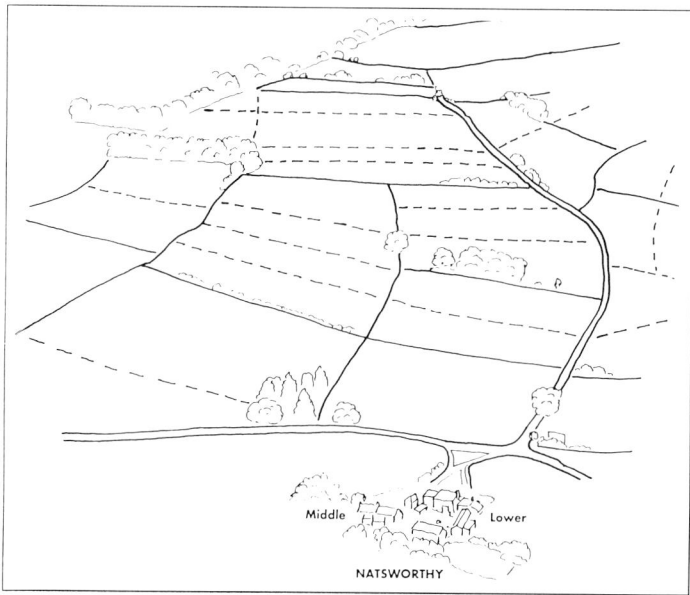

An aerial photograph, looking east, of Middle and Lower Natsworthy Farms and cottage, clearly shows the layout of the farm with the stripfields beyond. The dotted lines on the plan opposite indicate original stripfield boundaries that have been removed in modern times. The infield with its strips lies directly in front of the farms, with an access track running along its southern edge.

WIDECOMBE

BLACKSLADE AND DUNSTONE

'Ralph (de Pomeroy) has a manor called DUNESTANETUNA which Edwin held T.R.E. and it paid geld for half virgate. This one plough can till. Roger holds it of Ralf. On it Ro(ger) has 3 villeins and 4 bordars who have half plough, also 5 beasts, 3 sheep, 3 acres of meadow and 30 acres of pasture. Worth 7 shillings and 6 pence a year; when he received it 30 pence.'

'Along with this manor Ralf has a manor called BLACKESTAC (Exch. BLACKESTACH) which Edwit (Exch. Edwin) held T.R.E. and it paid geld for 1 virgate. This 1 plough can till. On it are 2 villeins and 3 bordars, also 2 acres of meadow. Worth 3 shillings a year.' - Domesday Book.

Blackslade today is still in the Dymond family and is today in the ownership of Mrs Anstice Brown who resides in Worcestershire. The farm's 100 acres are worked by Margaret and Aubrey Hares who run a beef herd of Friesian and Angus crosses. Both parties are in business together providing pony trekking and riding holidays.

The farm is in a beautiful setting, perched high on the valley side under Tunhill Rocks, with a sturdy track to the open moors above. The Dymond family always claimed they had the best view in the valley (disputed by others with similar panoramic views), although the windows of the manor house face away from the view - and away from the prevailing weather.

Above: an aerial view of Blackslade.

Below left: Blackslade Manor House and (**right**) a drawing of Blackslade dated 1867 before rebuilding took place. *(Dymond Diaries)*.

SAXON AND NORMAN SETTLEMENTS

The present hamlet of Lower Dunstone was formed on a Saxon manor owned by Edwin. Ralph de Pomeroy then received the estate from William I and it was held by the Hamlyn family for many centuries.

There were four farms in medieval times which may have been based on dwellings inhabited during Edwin's ownership. Francis (Frank) Hamlyn held one which he called Dunstone Court. Marriane Margaret (Mary) Hamlyn, on her inheritance, changed the name to Dunstone Manor, perhaps a more appropriate name on the evidence of Hutholes and other nearby Saxon manor settlements.

Lower Dunstone is the only farm surviving today, formerly known as Tollicks, a name dating from 1858 when John Tollick moved from the mill and bakery at Ponsworthy.

The third farm stood on the complex now known as Tremills, opposite a more modern building and the school room. The Tremills family is an ancient one in the parish with a long association with Dunstone.

The fourth farm, known as Wootens in the parish and manor accounts, does not exist today. The author's mother remembered its ruins lying behind Dunstone House which she saw built in 1930.

An aerial view of Lower Dunstone, site of a Saxon settlement.

Painting of Dunstone Manor by E.T. Holding c. 1920. This was before the present arched gateway was built (see over). Note the thatched barn, the roof of which collapsed in the 1930s.

WIDECOMBE

The arched entrance to Dunstone Court (now Manor), built by Mr Opie for Frank Hamlyn.

Above: Dunstone House c. 1920, from a postcard published by Owen Harvey at the Post Office, Widecombe. *(May Hambley)*.

Left: Lower Dunstone Farm.

Above: Tremills farmhouse, Lower Dunstone from a photograph believed to have been taken in the early 1920s. *(Iris Woods)*.

Left: Dunstone Cross, returned to its original site on Dunstone Green from the vicarage garden where it had been taken some years before.

SAXON AND NORMAN SETTLEMENTS

Following the Norman Conquest and on into the medieval period a pattern of farming known as the infield/outfield system was employed. Evidence of this remains clearly at Lower Dunstone. The farmers each had shared strips of land close to their farms on the watermeadows next to the Webburn. These were the infields. The outfields were larger blocks of land on the slopes of Hameldown.

One the fields is named 'Dowls', providing further evidence of this farming system. Hermon French suggests that this name derives from the OE *dal*, 'dole' in modern English, meaning a share or portion of land, especially a common field. It is possible that this pattern of farming and its fields system is based on the prehistoric reave system.

There was once a farm called North Dunstone which had a block of fields directly above the present road, with the manor boundary on one side and the access route 'Steep Lane' on the other. There is no indication of the original building but the lane has a curious bend in it and apple trees, growing here possibly indicate a former dwelling.

The aerial photograph and plan show clearly the infield/outfield system at Lower Dunstone. The broken lines on the plan indicate were field walls have been removed and the numbers indicate which fields belonged to which farm. No. 1 farm had been known as Wootens. No. 2 is Lower Dunstone, formerly Tollicks, which acquired North Dunstone lands (the block of fields marked 2 above the road). No 3 is Dunstone Court (now Manor). No 4 is known as Tremills.

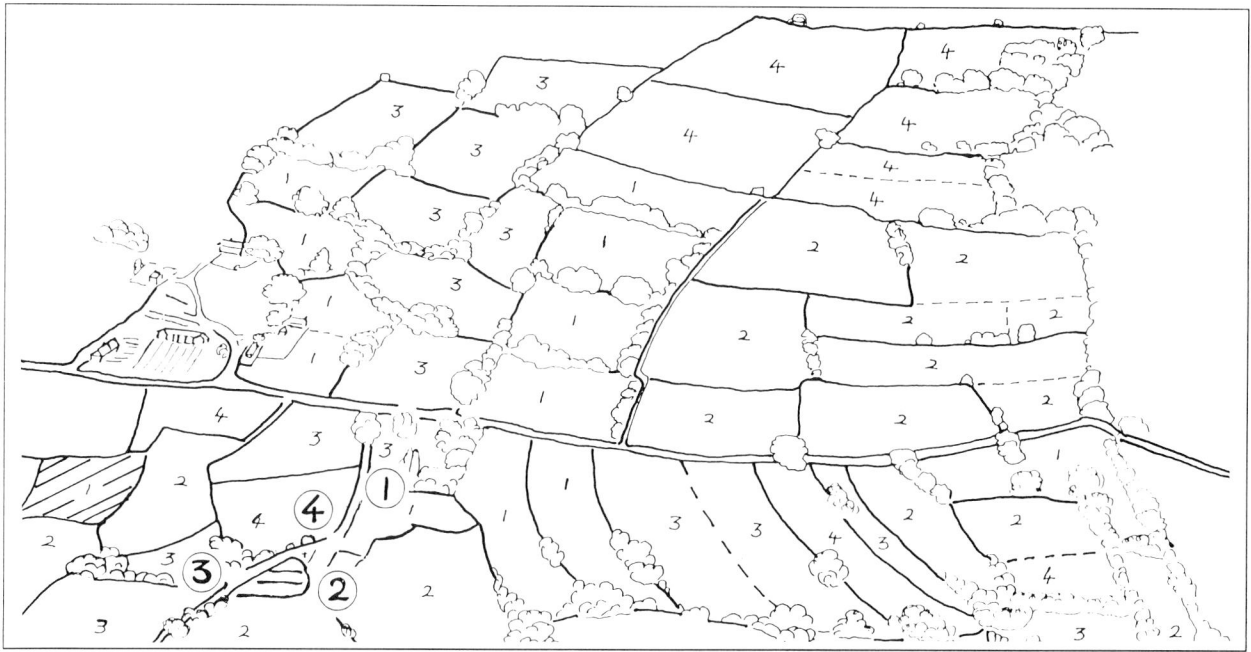

SCOBITOR

'The bishop (Bishop of Coutances) has a manor called Bovi... To this manor has been added the land of 15 thanes... A third is called SCABATORA (Exch. SCABATORE) and there 2 thanes were settled.' - Domesday Book.

The places mentioned in Domesday tend to be honoured with the title 'manor'. Blackslade was possibly an appendage to Dunstone Manor just as all the land held by thanes in Bovi were appendages to Bovi Manor. *The Place Names of Devon* records that Scobitor was mentioned in documents of c. 1200, 1219, 1388 and 1452. At some time it was owned by William de Bokelonde (Buckland - the neighbouring manor and parish) who on his death bequeathed it to Torre Abbey. There are three cartularies of that abbey, written in the first half of the thirteenth century, which refer to Scobitor: two of the charters are almost identical, the third is a quitclaim by Girard de Spineto. They are all written in Latin and the translation here is provided by Katherine Longley:

'Be it known to men present and to come that I, Roger de Bokelonde, have granted and given by this my present charter confirmed to God and the church of St Savior of Torr and the canons serving God there all the land of Scobitorr with all its appurtenances, in free, pure and perpetual alms, namely, that land which W. de Bokelonde my grandfather gave, together with his body, to the aforesaid church and canons.'

He went on to confirm 'reasonable common pasturage' and 'housebote and haybote in my wood of Hokemore', these being the rights to take timber for building and the right to gather wood for hedging.

The quitclaim of Girard de Spineto adds further information by telling us that Torre Abbey was to receive 'one ferling of land in Scobetorre which William de Bokelonde gave and bequeathed to the aforesaid canons together with his body.'

At the Dissolution of the Monasteries a great deal of property was acquired by Thomas Southcott, and he owned Scobitor in 1588. Richard Cabell owned the property in 1670 - he being the infamous wife-murderer whose hound is said to haunt the moor. This legend in turn gave birth to Conan Doyle's most famous work *The Hound of the Baskervilles*.

Though Cabell owned Scobitor, William Hamlyn was in occupation. He was followed by Hugh Hamlyn in 1702, who may also have been its owner. John Dunning purchased the property from Revd John Wooton, in 1769. Dunning was Solicitor General, later Lord Ashburton, and he bought three other Domesday manors, Blackslade, Natsworthy and Spitchwick. The Register of Baptisms in Widecombe records: 'Dunning, Richard Barre, second son of Lord Ashburton and Eliza, who was born at Spitchweek Park in the Parish half after two in the morning of Tuesday, the 17th of Septr, was baptised by me, John White, Curate of Withecombe. 15th Oct. 1782.'

Scobitor remained in Dunning's family, passing to his niece Margaret Baring in 1844. Ann Hamlyn was the tenant in 1780, to be followed by Thomas Hannaford in 1804 and Samual Hannaford in 1830 and 1844.

The farm was sold in 1867, 1909 and 1927, this last sale being to a Miss Penn-Gaskell it is believed. She was a friend of the author's grandparents.

In 1909 there were two dwellings on the site, so close together that one could pass one to the other through a door. It is intriguing that Domesday records 2 thanes settled here in 1087.

There was a great open fieplace with a traditional bread oven and the date 1725 was carved over the porch of the main dwelling.

The buildings have been extensively converted and restored since that date.

JORDAN

'William de Faleisa has a manor called CHOCHINTONA (Cockington) which Alric held T.R.E. and it paid geld for 3 hides... As a parcel of (de) the aforesaid 3 hides the same Alric held a manor called DEPDONA (Exch. DEPTONE) T.R.E. which paid geld for 1 virgate and has been added to the aforesaid manor. Worth 10 shillings; when W(illiam) received it the same. W(illiam) holds the two as one manor.' - Domesday Book.

For many years this manor was recorded as Dewdon and when it became Jordan is not known. It may well have been at Hutholes (see page 26), earlier known as South Rowden. As the land was cleared below and new settlements became established, the present Jordan may have captured the title 'manor'.

ORDINACIO DE LIDEFORD - AD 1260

The publication of a document on 20 August, 1260 proved to be crucial to the historical development of Widecombe. The issues contained in Bishop Bronscombe's *Ordinacio de Lideford* were to give Widecombe control over the inhabitants of the Ancient Tenements contained within the Royal Forest of Dartmoor which became known in Widecombe as The Forest Quarter.

The text of the original is here translated in full from the Latin by Katherine Longley:

The letter has been issued to all etc. The Bishop etc. Understanding from the statement of trustworthy persons that certain parishioners of the church of Lideford dwelling in the hamlets called Balbenye and Pushyll are at such a distance from the mother-church aforesaid that they are quite unable to attend it as often as they ought on account of great distance, we have given written instructions to our beloved son, the Official of the Archdeacon of Totnes, to hold a solemn inquiry in full chapter of the same place, and inform us in writing whether the men aforesaid are wealthy enough to build an oratory; also, whether the same men may hear divine service and receive the sacraments of the Church (there) without the prejudice of the right of another church; and what is the distance of the same hamlets from the mother-church aforesaid; and whether in times of storm and flood the same parishioners, wishing to attend the mother-church aforesaid, are obliged to take a longer route. And when we found, by the report of the Official aforementioned, that the same inhabitants having insufficient means to build an oratory, the parish church of Wydecombe is nearer than all the others to the same places, and that the places aforesaid are distant from the mother-church of Lideford by eight miles in fair weather and by a circuitous route of fifteen miles in times of storm, desiring by all means the salvation of souls, which we must not neglect, we had the rectors of the same churches summoned to our presence; the rectors aforesaid being therefore before us, and this danger being explained to them, and they submitting themselves (with the express permissions of the patrons of each church) to our ordination, and promising to comply in good faith with our will in this matter and to observe our ordination aforesaid in perpetuity, with the advice and assistance of judicious men we have ordained thus, namely, that while the inhabitants of the aforesaid places and of those adjacent shall remain for ever thus in the unity of their parish church of Lideford, they may in future hear divine service and receive all the Church's sacraments, for the living and the dead, in the church of Wydecombe. They may contribute to the (repair of the) roof and to the fabric of the church of Wydecombe, to the churchyard fence, the maintenance of lights and the receiving of blessed bread, together with those persons whose parish church it is; they may observe the customs of the same church in the visiting of the sick, the blessing of marriage-partners, purification after childbirth, baptism of infants, mortuary payments and burial of the dead, they may also make solemn offering there three times in the year, and nevertheless pay full tithe of lambs to the same church. As a token, however, of submission to and acknowledgement of the right of the parish, each Inhabitant of the said places who is a land-holder shall once in the year, namely on St Petroc's day, make solemn offering in the church of Lideford, and shall pay, without any diminution or gainsaying, all tithes and obventions, greater and lesser, to his mother-church of Lideford, with the sole exception of those mentioned above. In witness therefore etc...

WIDECOMBE

It has been stated that, on the evidence of the *Ordinacio de Lideford,* that Babeny and Pizwell (the two hamlets mentioned in the document), were the first and only ancient tenements at the time the document was published in 1260. As Bishop Bronscombe refers specifically to 'landowners' it can be assumed that the three farms at each establishment were in existence.

The Bishop also refers to the inhabitants of adjacent holdings, and although no documentary evidence exists for Brimpts, Runnage and Walna in 1260, they may well have been there some fifty years before the earliest record.

Above: An aerial view of Pizwell.

Left and below: The four farmhouses at Pizwell.

THE MANOR FARMS AND ANCIENT TENEMENTS

Freda Wilkinson has written a very informative account of two farms: Babeny (in *Dartmoor - A New Study*), and Lake (in *History of the Farm*). A study of the Dartmoor longhouse and farmstead was included in the author's previous work *Dartmoor Stone*, and the following information adds to these accounts in specific relation to Widecombe.

The listing below includes most of the farming hamlets; places where more than one farm occupied a site. The dates given are the earliest recorded reference to the site, not when they were built (for instance, the manors listed in Domesday were in the hands of Saxon owners before the Conquest).

FARMING HAMLETS

BITTLEFORD	956	SHERRIL	1301
NATSWORTHY	1086	NORTHWAY	1330
DUNSTONE	1086	SOUTHWAY	1330
BLACKSLADE	1086	UPPACOTT	1330
SPITCHWICK	1086	LANGWORTHY	1333
JORDAN	1086	HANAFORD	1333
SCOBITOR	1086	Hr.&Lr. AISH	1371
CATOR	1167	COMBE	1384
BLACKATON	1238	GRENDON	1505
Hr.&Lr. TORR	1249	ROWDEN	1545
VENTON	1249	BONEHILL	1652
ROWBROOK	1291		

INDVIDUAL FARMS

BARTON (NORTHALL)	1244	UPHILL	1330
CHITTLEFORD	1244	KINGHEAD	1333
STONE	c1250	LAKE	1333
TUNHILL	1253	HATCHWELL	1352
PONSWORTHY	1281	E SHALLOWFORD	1400
LEIGHTOR	1289	W SHALLOWFORD	1400
CORNDON	1303	LIZWELL	1443
PITTON	1311	SWEATON	1544
SOUTHCOMBE	1313	LEY	1566
OLDSBROOM	1317	ISEFORD	1566

The individual farms listed above all appear to have been single units. The vast majority of sites in both the above lists are still in occupation today though, in many cases, those in the first list have merged into single ownership, as have the Ancient Tenements. Along with the farms and hamlets, the parish contained scores of smallholdings and cottages making up an agricultural community.

THE ANCIENT TENEMENTS

BABENY	3	1260
PIZWELL	3	1260
HUCCABY	5	1296
RUNNAGE	2	1304 (includes
Warner/Walna)		1301 LOST
DUNNABRIDGE	4	1305
BRIMPTS	3	1307
SHERBERTON	3	1307
BROOM PARK	1	1307
HEXWORTHY	3	1317 (Hextenesworth)
DURY	1	1344
MERRIPIT (Lr.)	1	1344
BELLEVER	2	1355 (includes
Lake/Hevede)		1347 LOST
RIDDON	1	1488
HARTLAND	1	1521
PRINCE HALL	1	1521
BROWN BERRY	1	1563

These farming communities were founded inside the Royal Forest and, from Bishop Bronscombe's decree of 1260, they formed the Forest Quarter of Widecome Parish.

It is interesting to speculate on the origin of some of these place names, especially in relation to the older family names in the parish. Hamlyn has been dealt with elsewhere in this book but Hermon French suggests that Hannford comes from 'Hanna's Worthy' and it is possible that this large family descended from this single farmstead. Similarly, the Hext(e)s come from Hexworthy, for we have recorded Robert Hexta of Hextesworthy (1417), founder of the family who thrived in the parish for over 500 years.

After the Norman Conquest it was common that names would be set down as 'Christian name de establishment'; this lasting for the next 400 years, for example: Roger de Spitchwick, Ralph de Uppecote, Wills de Meripitt, Johes de Ollesbrom.

WIDECOMBE

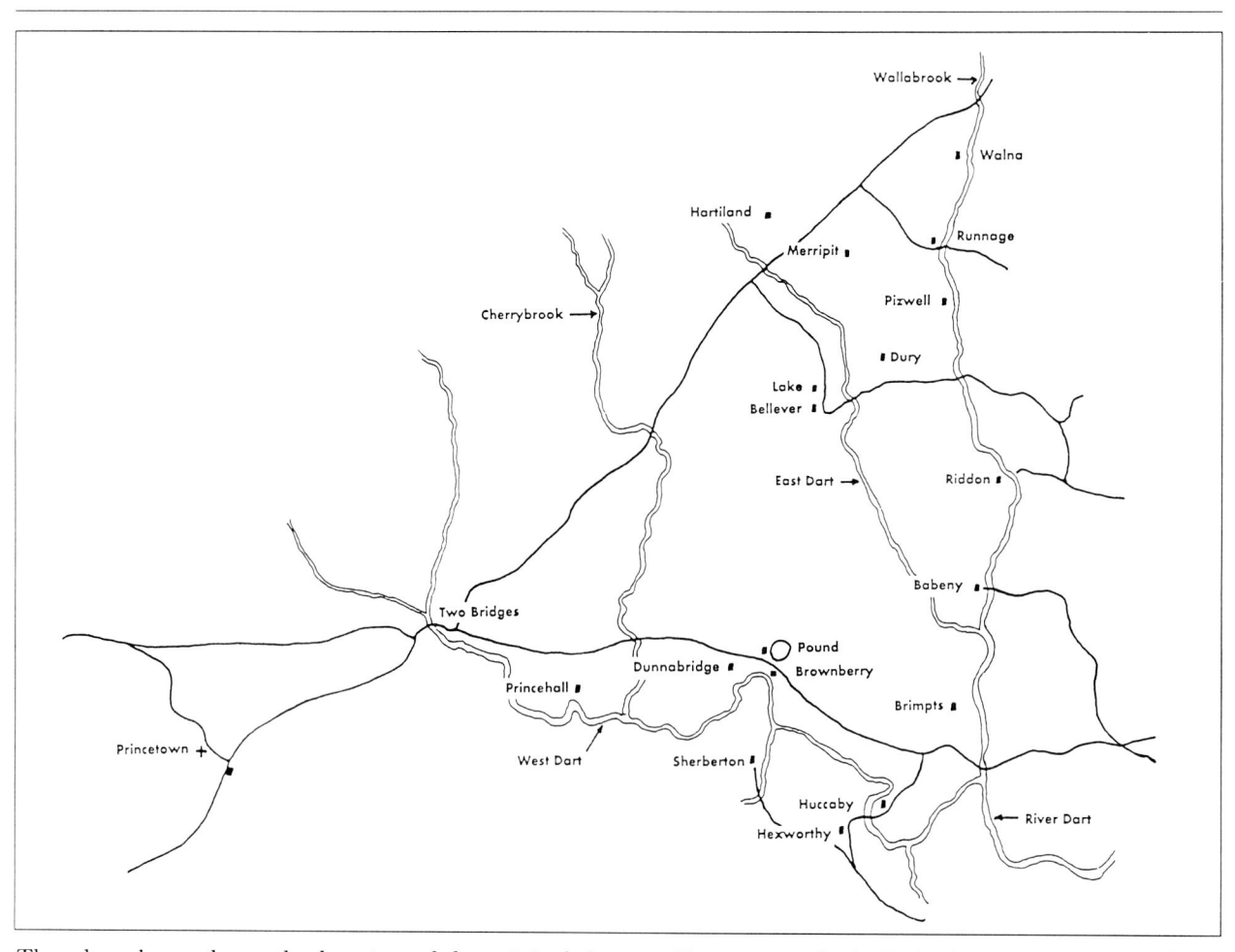

The plan above shows the location of the original Ancient Tenements of which the layout of Uppacot (seen below) is typical in its clustered grouping of buildings.

THE MANOR FARMS AND ANCIENT TENEMENTS

FARMING HAMLETS

Bittleford Farm 1908: from W.R. Gay's postcard series. *(Ena Prowse)*.

Above: Higher Sherill Farm c. 1920 (now shown as Sherwell on OS maps. *(Iris Woods)*.

Above: Lower Torr Farm. *(Iris Woods)*.

Above: Higher Uppacot as it appeared in the early years of this century and (**left**) a recent photograph of the same view which shows remarkably little change.

WIDECOMBE

INDIVIDUAL MANOR FARMS

Lizwell Farm 1908: from W.R. Gay's postcard series. *(Ena Prowse)*.

Right: Corndonford Farm has an imposing porchway with inscribed lintel (see opposite).

Tunhill Farm.

THE MANOR FARMS AND ANCIENT TENEMENTS

Top left: doorway arch at Corndonford Farm, inscribed R.W. 1718.

Top right: a similar porch at Chittleford Farm, dated 1680.

Left: Red Devon cattle graze at Ponsworthy Farm c. 1910. *(Marjorie and Geoff Weymouth).*

Below: Ollsbrim Farm

THE ESTATE OF LANO DE CADETREW

The Domesday manors were established by 1087 but it was not for many centuries that the land boundaries as we know them today were documented. Within the present manor of Spitchwick a large estate was formed on today's Cators sometime prior to 1245. This is set out in a document which is a later copy of the original:

I Thomas de Spicwyk have granted and confirm to Gilbert son of Lano de Cadetrew and his heirs 2 ferlings of land in Chadetrew which Michael my father gave to Lano his father with An ... his daughter and my sister in free marriage with these bounds namely:
from Weiebourne as to the lands of William de Dawedunn extending as far as the corner of the meadow Churtais and in line as far as the Pikestann above the back of the hill at Holeshafde and in line to the lands of Warin son of Joel extending as far as the Fenniw Ford and in line as far as Didelake hafde and in line to the Pikedstanne on Chokeard and in line to the land of William Giffard extending as far as Wedeburne.

John Somers Cocks assisted by Hermon French studied this grant and the author is indebted to JSC for his notes and sketch map upon which the material here is based.

There are at least two interesting points to note from the grant: firstly the number of named bounds which are still in use today, and the recording of two sett stones included in the bounds. Whether these latter were set up as part of the grant or whether they already existed as bound marks is not known.

JSC wrote 'I enclose a rough plan of the Cator Bounds c. 1260 as I think them to have been. There is slight doubt as there always is in places with these old bounds, but I don't think they are far wrong.'

To perambulate these bounds we start from the banks of the West Webburn and follow the common boundary of the two Lower Cators (one of which was held by William de Dawedunn, member of the family of the Domesday manor of Dewdon), until we reach the 'corner of the meadow of Churtais' which may have been the last field enclosed against the open commons.

These 'common' walls are interesting insofar as they are often built on the foundations of prehistoric reaves.

The next named point on the boundary is 'Holeshafde' on the line to the 'Pikestann' and here we have a field name to confirm the bound, Cater Hall or Hole (previously Holes Head). The Pikestann is still in place.

We now cross over Corndon Down, past the lands of Warin son of Joel, to Fennie Ford. JSC gives credit to Hermon French for finding two sets of stones which establish the line over the Down. At Fennie Ford is the well-documented Leapyeat, Venniford Gate. This was the gateway into the Royal Forest and, in medieval times, those responsible for its upkeep were often fined for being derelict in their duties.

We now follow the Wallabrook to 'Horebrygge Ford', a name which is no longer with us, but the course of a stream which only flows in wet seasons, Deadlake, does run down to the Wallabrook near Riddon and is the common boundary of Middle and Great Cator farms.

It would be difficult to establish 'Horebrygge Ford' as the tinners have used the Wallabrook hereabouts in search of tin and in at least two points the river's course is changed almost ninety degrees.

From 'Didlake Head' we walk to the 'Pikedstanne on Chokerand' The steep hill road west of Middle Cator is still known as Coakers Hill. This puts the Pikedstanne somewhere on Cator Green, a triangle of grass unfenced until recent times where lately a stone has been set to mark the approximate position of the missing 'stanne'.

The boundary then passes to Clampitte, now lost, and beside the 'Corndyche' down to the Webburn. We have seen that the boundary follows the bound of Middle and Great Cator along the Deadlake so it seems safe to suggest that William Giffard owned the land not held by Great Cator and his boundary was the cornditch, another common wall, running parallel to the one followed at the start of this perambulation.

The 'Pikestann' above Lower Cator, the bound described in Lano de Cadetrew's thirteenth-century estate grant.

THE ESTATE OF LANO DE CADETREW

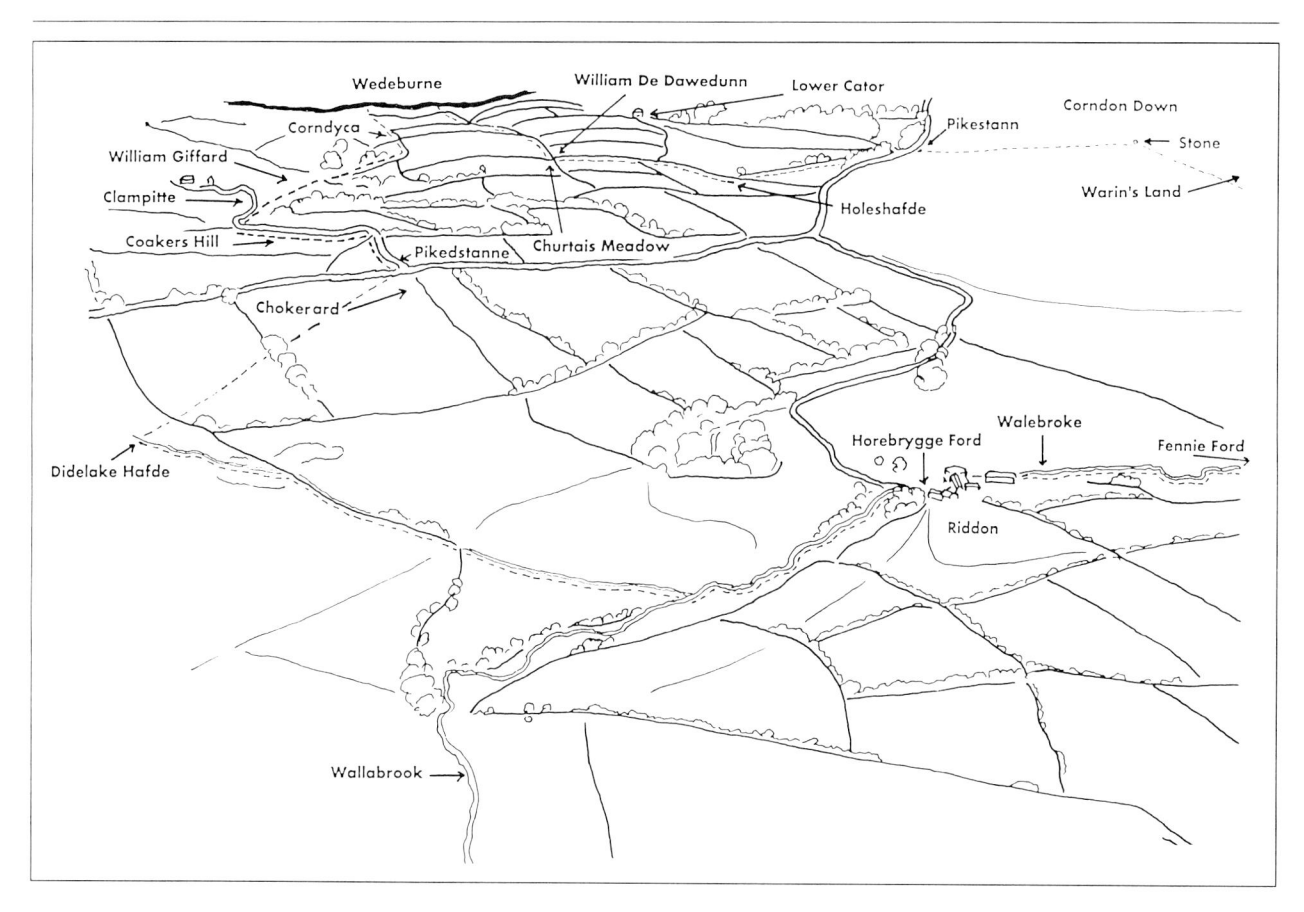

The plan above and the corresponding aerial photograph below provide details of the original estate boundary as defined in the grant of land to Lano de Cadetrew by Thomas de Spicwyk c. 1260. The drawing is taken from information provided by the late John Somers Cocks.

DUNSTONE COTTAGE

Along with the farm dwellings, whether grouped or sited singly, there are in the parish numerous cottages, originally the homes of artisans and labourers.

The Revd L.J. McCrea, the author's grandfather, bought one such cottage at Dunstone and the family were in occupation for sixty-eight years. It is impossible to say exactly when it was built but it is likely this occurred in the early 1800s, at about the time the Parish Cottages were extended.

The original Parish Cottage was used as support to the Church House, as the churchwardens' accounts report, on 6 September, 1822: 'John Rendle to have a bed in the Poor House at Dunstone and Ann Potter to come back to Widecombe Poor House to go round from Farm to Farm for daily labour and a shilling a week for Sunday's diet.'

On 7 October, 1825: 'The present meeting have come to a unanimous opinion to build two cottages at Dunstone adjoining to the east end of the present parish house - the rooms not to be less than 12 ft. square but to exceed 12 ft. in breadth if the present old house is broader - so as to make the front and back walls of the new and old house true linable, the ground room to be 7ft. high and the walls 5 ft. high above the chamber floor - a specification and estimate is required from any mason and carpenter willing to execute the work - the chamber to be lath and plastered a laths length in height above the wall. Tenders to be given in to the Church Wardens for the mason's and carpenter's work immediately.'

27 January, 1826: ' By direction of the Vestry Meeting, John Cleave to be paid on account of the cottages building at Dunstone fifteen pounds.' (He was to be paid £45 in all).

These cottages were probably built from materials of the ruined Lady House, originally a chapel and long since lost, which lay at one end of Lady Meadow. Numbers 1 to 4 Parish Cottages are still occupied today.

Records show that Dunstone Cottage, which was a separate building, was sold in 1834 and 1844. In 1852 D. Townsend and others sold it to Miss A. and Mr N. Smerdon for £137.10. Mr W.G. Gray and others conveyed it to Mr G. French in 1882 for £135, and it was sold again in 1909 to Francis (Frank) Hamlyn for £220, who sold it to the Revd Leonard James McCrea in 1920 for £1250. In 1960 it passed to his daughter Iris Marion Woods, the author's mother.

When Frank Hamlyn offered it for sale a number of people wanted to buy the cottage and the adjoining fields known as the Willow Pieces (see page 25) which Frank did not want to sell. My grandfather simply sent a telegram 'Money in Widecombe Post Office 8.30 tomorrow.' A single word reply 'Done!'

My mother sold the cottage by public auction, held in the Church House, on 11 November 1988. A cottage that had been built for £50 or so was finally knocked down on a bid of £153 000.

Cottages such as Dunstone had rights attached to them, not to the person who occupied or owned the cot, and thus Iris Woods registered under the Commons Registration Act 1965, her 'rights of common.' These included the rights of turbary - the right to dig peat or turf; the right of estovers - being the right to take tree loppings, gorse or furze, bushes or underwood; the right of pannage - the right to turn out pigs to eat acorns and beechmast.

In filling in the forms she also included the traditional cottager's rights: the right to pasture a broodmare or foal until the foal is weaned; the right to pasture one pig; the right to pasture one goose.

Such rights were jealously guarded by the commoners at the Manor Court. The Court and Homage for Dunstone would be opened on Dunstone Green and by tradition 'Chief Rents' would be paid at the Dun Stone before adjourning to Blackslade where the Jury would confirm all its ancient rights and look at any matters brought before it.

It may be thought that such rights, in existence for centuries, were well-established and beyond dispute, but a letter sent to the author's mother suggests otherwise:

"Objector No 476: His Royal Highness, Prince of Wales, Duke of Cornwall. Grounds: That the right of pannage does not exist on that part of the land comprised in this register..."

The area concerned was land on the edge of Dunstone Down, where doubtless few if any trees grew in historic times. Concerned that the young and virile heir-to-the-throne was about to do battle with my aging mother I asked her what she did - to which she smiled and replied: 'I withdrew!'

Early in 1990 I scattered my mother's ashes on Hameldown under whose shoulder she had lived for many years. Walking up the old Church Path from Pizwell I wondered how many others had toiled along this ancient route, carrying their loved ones to their final resting place.

DUNSTONE COTTAGE

Above: Higher Dunstone with Lady Meadow in the centre and the Poor House in the foreground. Dunstone cottage with the Methodist Chapel stand on the right and Berrywood at the top of the photograph. The house on the extreme left was built for the District Nurse with land taken from Chapel Field.

Left: Dunstone Cottage c, 1930. The lean-to earth closet was later removed.

Below left: feeding chickens and a pig at Dunstone c. 1920. The child is possibly Dorothy Miners (née Parsons), Bill Miners' sister. *(Thirza Nosworthy).*

Below: Great Dunstone Farm with Dunstone Cottage in the background. *(Marjorie and Geoff Weymouth).*

45

THE GLEBE FARM AND VICARAGE

Standing on the south side of the church tower looking down you see the land that Roger, son of Sir Ralph le Rous, sold to the church in 1283. Here, close to the road, stands Glebe Farm from which the vicar derived some of his income.

In 1815 the Glebe lands were the fields behind the forge and Old Inn that ran westward up the flank of Hameldown, bounded by the Churchway, an ancient track to Pizwell. This track may have been marked by a stone incised with a cross which now forms a gatepost at the entrance to the nearby lane to Kingshead Farm (see page 131). Included among the fields was an orchard.

Backing on to the Glebelands is the Parson's Barn where the vicar kept the produce of the church tithes. Beyond the Glebe stands the vicarage itself, rebuilt in the eighteenth century and remodelled in the following century, its cellars are part of the original dwelling and are possibly unique on Dartmoor.

The cellars are entered by a flight of steps from the rear of the house. Close to this entrance is a well, the water in which is some depth from the surface, otherwise the cellar would have been impossibly damp - perhaps even prone to flooding. The cellar stairs and walls are of rough granite. Two short passages link the three rooms which presently comprise the cellar area. The ceiling over the passageways and the door lintels are granite slabs.

One room has a bare wooden ceiling - the floor of the room above - which is now supported by a modern steel girder. The other two rooms are now brick-lined and arched, as would be a wine cellar. William Crossing says of the Revd James Holman Mason, he was famous for his hospitality and the 'excellence of his port'.

One fascinating feature of the cellars is a neat granite window set in a rough stone wall at one end of one of the brick-lined rooms. The window is about 30 inches square and has chamfered granite surrounds and centre-post, complete with a vertical iron bar set central in the left-hand opening. Through this window it is possible to see another set of granite steps running parallel to those descending from the entrance. From this it might be surmised that there were originally two dwellings on this site, each with its own cellar - the vicar living in the larger dwelling, his servants next door.

It is possible to see signs of the renovations of past years by walking around the outside of the property. The revd J.P. Jones, writing in 1828, records: 'The Vicarage House has recently undergone extensive repairs - on an old beam were found the letters HMB in Lombardic capitals, possibly referring to Henricus Magister Brusee, Vicar of Widecombe 1503-1532.'

Outside the vicarage is a very fine upping stock, with the village well across the road.

The mysterious underground window in the Vicarage cellars.

THE GLEBE FARM AND VICARAGE

Left: the Glebe Farm. *(Iris Woods)*.

Below: field names of the Glebe lands as shown on the tithe apportionment. This document laid out the annual value of the lands.

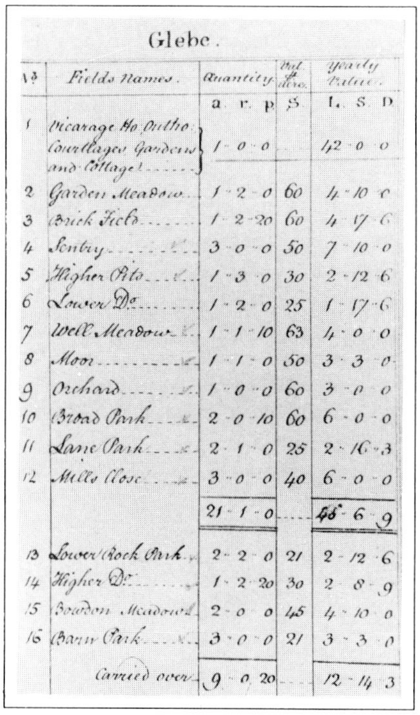

Above: the Vicarage. The present building dates from around 1820 although the cellars are at least early sixteenth century.

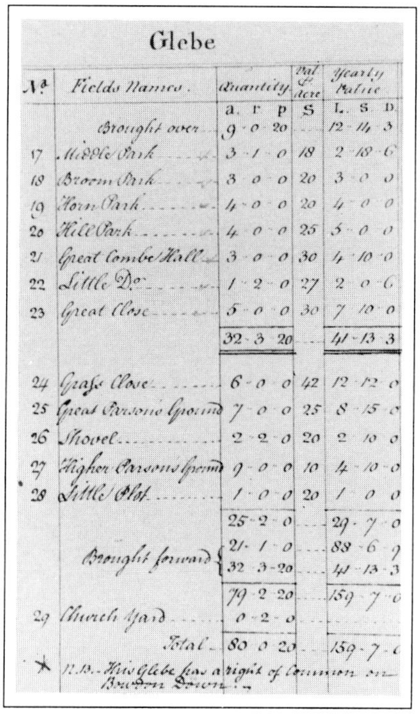

Right: granite steps descending into the vicarage cellars.

47

An aerial view of St Pancras church and churchyard. The Church House lies beneath the shadow of the tower and the vicarage can be seen centre right at the bottom of the photograph.

THE CATHEDRAL OF THE MOOR

Widecombe Church is aptly described as 'The Cathedral of the Moor'. It dominates the village and stands majestically in its moorland setting.

The earliest document referring to a church is Bishop Bronscombe's *Ordinacio de Lideford*, dated 1260 (see paged 35). The list of Rectors predates this document, beginning in 1253 with 'unknown' and continuing:

 1258 Master Thomas de Bokelonde
 1278 Master Roger Le Rous
 1280 John Fitz Richard

At this time Sir Ralph Fitz Richard of Widecombe Town Manor owned North Hall.

Another early document dated 1283 is, according to Dymond: 'A deed under which Roger, Son of Sir Ralph le Rous, of an ancient family seated at Modbury, sold to the Dean and Chapter of Exeter an acre of land, at Wydecombe, with the advowson of the Church of St Pancras. The acre of land is described as adjacent to the Mother Church of the Parish and is lying in Wodehay (now Wooda or Wooder) hard by the sanctuary of the church and extending lengthwise from the West as far Eastward as the part of the said sanctuary highway leading from the church towards Dunsterton [Dunstone].'

In medieval times the church was a refuge for the oppressed and the sanctuary of the church also included the land outside the building itself. At Widecombe this included the graveyard running down towards the banks of the Webburn - taking its modern name The Sentry from 'sanctuary'. The acre of land which Roger Le Rous sold to the church is that land upon which the Glebe Farm, Parson's Barn and the Vicarage now stand - it may also have included part of the brickfield.

In 1406, John Shillingford, Canon of Exeter, expressed in his will the wish to be buried in the Chapel of St Catherine, in the parish church of Widecombe, next to his mother. This is further unequivocal documentary evidence that a place of worship existed at Widecombe before the present church was built. It is likely that this earlier structure was of timber construction.

The stone built body of the church is medieval, but the church tower was built many years afterwards. It is known that the Church House was built around 1638 and, from a comparison of the masonry it is safe to assume that the church tower was also built at this time. Bridget Cherry states that 'nowhere else in Devon can the typical South West English contrast between tower and church be seen so uncompromisingly'.

An earlier architectural historian, James Hine, writing in 1874, states: 'Widecombe Church is throughout Perpendicular in style, the eastern portions of early character for the most part, the tower and much of the work in the north and south aisles, including the square-headed windows, late Perpendicular.' Of the moulded wooden arches to the north and south chantries, Hine says 'they are unique features which should be carefully preserved.'

The tower, though not typically Devonian, epitomises all the beauty that we associate with English country churches. Various authorities quote differing heights for the tower but John L. Webber, the nineteenth-century village constable, wrote a poem describing how he and the vicar measured the height with a plumbline, and quotes a height of 135 feet. The flat lead roof of the tower was renewed in 1747, as the names of the churchwardens inscribed there testify. Others have since left there own mark on the roof, including those who drew around their foot, writing their initials within the outline.

It is frequently stated that the tower was built by the tinners of the district, or at least that they provided the funds. There appears to be no direct evidence of this although the list of those paying coinage duty at Ashburton contains a number of Widecombe family names: Frenche, Caunter, Hext, Hamlyn, Nosworthy and Smerdon.

Other tinners were John Langworthy of Rowdon; John Langworthy of Southcombe; John Mann of Sherwill; John Wyndeat of Wethcomb; John Leyman of Pansforthe. Duty on smelted tin was also paid by the church of St Pancras itself.

It would seem that at about the time the tower was built there was a church guild or investment in the tin industry and it is more likely that this was the source of finance for the church tower.

Over the centuries the tower has withstood the continuous onslaught of nature. Recent reparations have undone much of the erosion caused by the climate over the years, and has eradicated the traces of the damage done by the storm of 1638 and the earthquake of 1752.

It was during Sunday afternoon service on 21 October 1638 that a tornado, accompanied by lightning hitting the tower, brought down the north-east pinnacle. The masonry fell through the roof causing death and injury to those present.

Polwhele reports 'There were in all four persons killed, and sixty two hurt,' though some accounts give a higher death toll. Full details of the tragedy were published in a tract *A True Relation of those strange and lamentable Accidents, happening in the Parish Church of Wythecombe in Devonshire on Sunday the 21st October 1638* by Master Wykes and Master Rothwell, Wardens.

Originally published on 17 November, the morbid curiousity of the population was satisfied only by the republishing of the tract on 19 and 27 November. Only two of those who died are mentioned by name: Master Hill and Robert Meade, the 'Warriner'.

The register of burials for that year lists fifteen names up to 13 October followed by:

Hill, Roger, gent	*23 October*
Meade, Robertt	*23 October*
Milward, Sibella	*23 October*
Hamlyn, Susan (wife of James)	*23 October*
Sheere, Walter	*1 November*
Beard, Bridgett Wid.	*6 November*

No further burials are recorded until 31 January 1639 and it might be assumed that those named above were also victims of the storm. Sibella Milward might be 'the maid from Manaton' described in the tract as 'visiting a friend'. Bridgett Beard might be the 'ancient woman' whose horrifying injuries are described at length.

The tract records that on the day following the storm 'thousands more witnesses' came to 'view the ruins of the church'. At the burial services of Hill and Meade the minister read the burial service and threw a handful of earth on to the coffins 'the fall whereof making a sudden noise made them all in great fear runne out of the Church, tumbling over one another, supposing the Church was falling on their heads...'

Of the tragedy itself Polwhele records that 'a long description by the rustic muse of Widecombe is hung against the north wall to the admiration of parishioners.' This poetic treatment on wooden panels is said to be the work of Richard Hill, village schoolmaster and son of Roger Hill. The original boards were renewed in 1786 by the churchwardens Peter and Sylvester Mann and hung on the wall of the tower.

The tower was to receive another knock from nature as the antiquarian Mrs Eliza Bray was to record: 'The last convulsion of any extraordinary character occurred in the year 1752, when, on the 23rd day of February, a smart shock of an earthquake was felt at many places on the moor, and its immediate neighbourhood - Manaton, Moreton Hampstead and Widdecombe. In the last named village some houses were injured and one of the pinnacles of the tower of the church was thrown down.' The churchwardens' accounts of 1751 record: 'Charles Stanbury's Bill of day's work at 1/4 the day £3.5.2.' He was the skilled workman who repointed the tower and replaced the pinnacle.

The structure of the church had deteriorated before the Dymonds bought Dunstone Manor and Blackslade in the mid nineteenth century. Robert Dymond edited his book published in 1876 with the intention of raising money for much needed restoration. He says 'The edifice was in a truly dreadful state of disrepair. The roof, neither wind nor water tight, was feebly upheld by rotting rafters. The distorted tracery of the granite windows could scarcely retain their leaded panes. Green streaks showed where the driving rain had trickled down the wall. To judge by appearances the whitewashers had been the only artificers employed there for many long years.'

So bad were conditions that the churchwardens had daubed in whitewash above the south porch the text: 'How dreadful is this place'.

In 1873 the Dymond diaries recorded that the 'service was shortened by the omission of the Litany... and Mr Williams announced that owing to the state of the church it was unsafe for the congregation to remain there longer... The state of the church was indeed deplorable for all the western end of the nave was open to the sky and a large hole in the roof of the north transept rendered our seat at any rate more airy than was comfortable.'

Although the churchwardens' accounts prior to this time are full of entries recording expenditure on the fabric of the church, little was done other than cosmetic repairs: '1741, Pd. Henry Mudge of Dean Prior for new painting and writing down 4 sentences in ye Church at 10/6 each £2.2.0.' and '1766 Pd. John Doble for gilt for the Angle [angel] etc. which was omitted last year £1.1.0.'

The churchwardens were responsible to the Archdeacon at Exeter for the maintenance of the church's fabric, except the chancel, for provision of material, utensils, books for use at services, allocation of seating, and the upkeep of churchways and the churchyard. They were also bound by oath to report on the performance of the incumbent, and to bring forward any moral or religious delinquency among the people.

That the wardens took their civic duties seriously can be seen from the many entries recorded in the accounts: '1722 Pd. for a warrant to those p'sons that wached by ye waterside to keep out ye ships that came beyond whare the plage was,' and '1750 Pd. for killing a doge which made a Great Decimation among Ews and lambs and the like £1.10.0d.'

It was by no means all hard work, however: '1713 Beer for ringers and wood for bonfire when peace

THE CATHEDRAL OF THE MOOR

Left: the tower of Widecombe church.

Below: two illustrations relating the effects of the storm of 1638. The top picture dates from 1684 and was published as the frontispiece to *The Widecombe Tracts* by James and Commin, 1905. The lower picture is possibly contemporary with the storm, also published in *The Widecombe Tracts*.

Above left: a photograph taken in 1910 showing the interior of the church - note the Ten Commandments hanging on each side of the altar,

Left: graffiti on the lead roof of the church.

51

WIDECOMBE

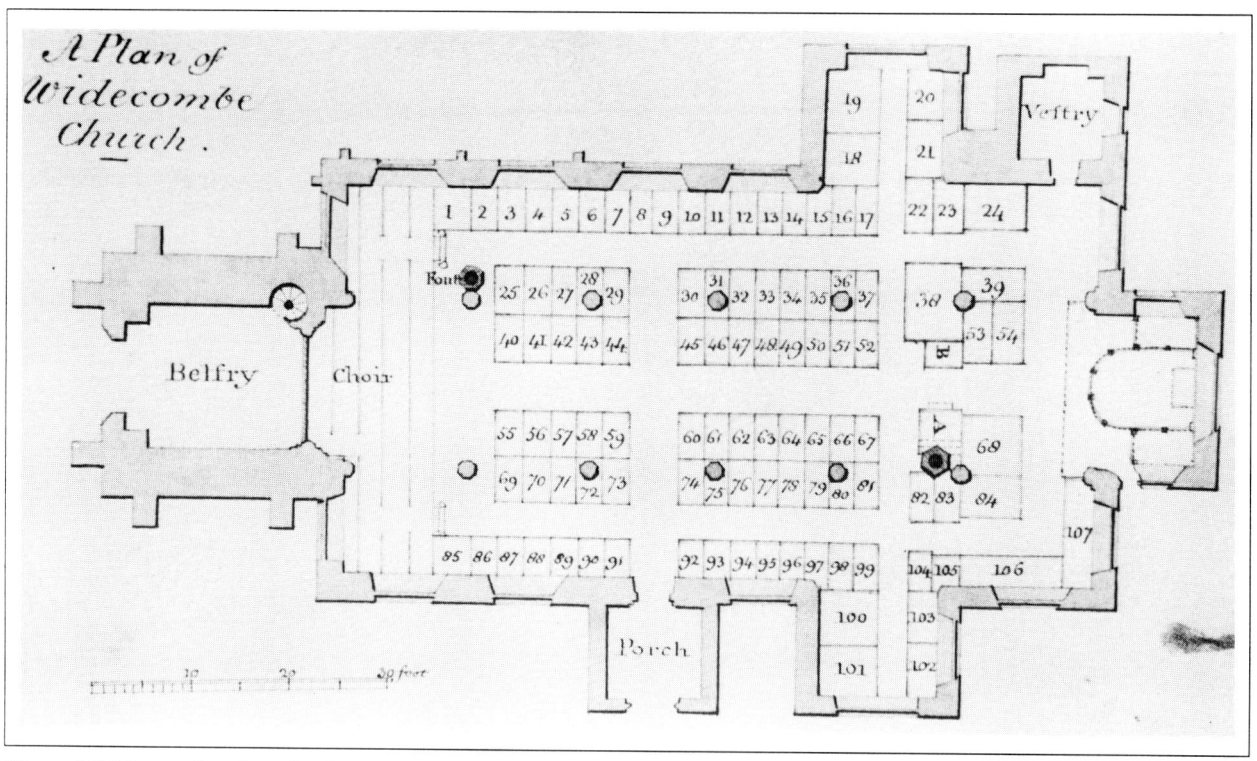

Plan of Widecombe church detailing the pews and boxes and their occupants in 1815. These seating arrangements were removed in the renovations of the 1870s. *(Keith Fox).*

LIST OF SEATING PLACES IN WIDECOMBE CHURCH, 1815

A. The Clergyman's Desk
B. The Clerk's ditto
1. Seat for the Butts or Hassocks
2.
3. } Vacant seats
4.
5.
6. Seats for any persons
7.
8.
9. Mrs White of Stone
10. Poundsgate
11. Womens seats
12. Cater
13. Lower Cater
14. Mr Langdon for Little Cater
15.
16. Young men any persons
17.
18. Nich' Smerdon
19. Farmers Servants
20. Babeny Servants
21. Mr French of Babeny
22. Wm Mann of Blackslade
23. Broadaford
24. For labouring men
25. Seats occupied by Christenings
26.
27. } Vacant seats
28.
29. Jourdan
30. Hatchwill
31. A Vacant seat
32. Natsworthy
33. Cater
34. Mr H. French of S. Natsworthy
35. Thos May of Sherwill
36. Occupied by any person
37. The Farmer of Glebe
38. Spitchwick
39. Kingshead, Great Cater & Brimpts
40.
41. For Poor People
42. Womens seats
43. Combe and Bunhill
44. Southway
45. Mrs Arnold for Sweaton
46. Rowdon
47. Dockwill
48. Chittleford & Hill
49. Rowdon
50. Shallaford & Hill
51. Isaford
52. Huccaby and Northway
53. Vicarage Servants
54.
55. } Poor people - Women
56.
57.
58. Kingshead & Upacot
59. Ash & Lower Dunstone
60. Babeny
61. Dunstone & Bittleford
62. Venton
63. Dockwill
64. Dunstone & Bittleford
65. Grendon
66. John White for Pitton
67. Wm Langdon Sen' Chittleford
68. Vicarage Pew
69. Daughters of Tradesmen
70.
71. Northway
72. Chittleford
73. Blackslade
74. Dury
75. Jourdan Mills
76. Scobator & Blackdon
77. Holwell (Mannaton)
78. Stranger's Seat
79. Samuel Wills of Wooder
80. Hatchwill
81. Lower Ash
82. Sercombe
83. Drywill & East Shollaford
84. Northall
85.
86.
87. } Vacant seats
88.
89.
90.
91. Sexton
92.
93. Poor women
94.
95. School Master
96. Bunhill & Dunnabridge
97. John Smerdon of Bunhill
98. Hannaford & Dunnabridge
99. Bittleford
100. Lizwell
101. Lizwell Servants
102. Vacant seat
103. Tradesmen
104. Venton
105. Sweaton
106. Stone
107. Young men

was proclaimed,' and '1727 Pd. Expenses when the King was crowned, Henry White for beer and bread £1.15.6d, John Nosworthy for victuals 11.6d.'

The chancel was the hallowed ground of Christian faith and worship, the remainder of the church was what we would call today the 'community centre'. This provided space for dancing, plays, feasts, even elections and meetings of the parishioners. The churchwardens of Ashburton in their accounts gave 2 shillings towards 'Crysmas games played in the church.'

In order to protect the sanctity of the chancel a rood screen was built across the church and the screen door was kept locked. Above the screen was the rood loft which housed the cross or 'rood' that stood above the doors. Access to the loft in Widecombe church was provided by a fine set of stone steps, the newell staircase, and a neat granite archway.

The screen itself became much decayed and only a small part of it now remains. This comprises a series of paintings of saints and ecclesiastical figures on wooden panels. The paintings themselves are much disfigured, said by some to be the work of puritans during Cromwell's time, showing their disdain for such 'idolatry'.

The damage might as easily be attributed to vandalism in any other period when one considers the uses to which the church was submitted. Even animals were no strangers to the church; in the great storm of 1638 'one man going out of the chancel door, his dog ran before him, who was whirled about towards the door and fell stark dead.'

Betwen 1720 and 1730 Mary Mann was paid five shillings a year for 'sweeping the church', and the same amount 'for keeping out the dogs.'

The costs of repairs to the remaining fabric of the church, its slate roof, the leaded windows, are all meticulously recorded in the accounts. These records provide a fascinating glimpse of the church of St Pancras over the centuries and bring to life the importance of that building to the parishioners past and present.

A section of the rood screen.

WIDECOMBE

Top row (l-r): St Catherine of Alexandria; Christ in Glory; Matthew's Man, or John the Baptist; **(2nd row):** green man; winged head; tinners' rabbits; **(3rd row):** dove of peace (or eagle representing St John the Evangelist); the pelican in piety; the yale; **(bottom row):** badge of Edward IV (1461-83); tree of life; The Holy Ghost or Crown of Thorns.

WIDECOMBE CHURCH BOSSES

The medieval church builders covered the joints of the roof beams with carved and painted wooden plaques, or bosses as they are more correctly known. These carvings often follow a religious theme, though this may also include references to pre-Christian icons.

Other themes are heraldic - usually with reference to local figures of importance, or national heroes. These themes become intermingled in some cases, often deliberately, and there is much humour and artistic licence to be found among the images.

It is much to be regretted that a number of the old bosses in Widecombe have decayed, although the church still has a very fine collection. Among those lost are a griffin, the white hart of Richard II (1377-1399), and a variety of heads.

There is an immediate connection between the boss of St Catherine (St Katharine of Alexandria) and the church, as described on page 57. This saint, martyred in the fourth century, and said to be of noble birth, protested against the persecution of the Christians.

She was tortured on the wheel and, legend has it, the wheel broke, injuring many of the watching crowd. She was then beheaded and milk flowed from the wound. She is patron saint of trades based on wheels, milling, and spinning. The boss shows her holding the martyrs' sword, while the wheel, on the right-hand side, has buckets like those of a waterwheel.

The boss showing three rabbits (or hares?) is well-known locally and much has been written about its symbolic significance. Similar designs are to be found in the churches of North Bovey, Chagford, South Tawton, Sampford Courtenay, Spreyton and Tavistock. It is said that the hare was the alchemists' symbol for tin and the design is known as the tinners' rabbits. Other interpretations are that the rabbits represent the Trinity and in this manner it is known as the Hunt of Venus.

The demi figure of Christ in Glory is easily recognised and requires no explanation. Other heads are less easily identified - the superb bearded head could be John the Baptist or St Matthew, known symbolically as Matthew's Man. This latter carving is remarkably similar to three stone carvings found in the windows, one in the north chantry aisle chapel, and two in the chancel window. It is likely that all four carvings are by the same person.

The foliate heads, those which have tendrils growing from mouths and nostrils, are derived from the pagan figure 'Jack in the Green', a favourite at May Day celebrations.

The bird figure can be viewed either as an eagle or a dove (the dove of peace). The eagle represents one of the four living creatures in the Book of Revelations and represents St John the Evangelist.

The 'pelican in piety' is always shown with its young at its breast. It is likely that in this case the carver had never seen such a bird - it looks rather like a swan - but it's symbolic meaning is synonymous with Christ's sacrifice and redemption.

The lion rampant is a representation of St Mark - but also is the king's beast and appears on the coat of arms of the first Duke of Cornwall.

The antelope, or more correctly the mystical yale of bestiary, has long serrated horns which are entangled in undergrowth. In heraldic design it has tusks like a boar and wears a chain around its neck. The beast appeared on the arms of Henry IV (1399-1413) and his descendants. John Russell, Duke of Bedford, received Tavistock Abbey at the Dissolution and it may be this connection that is reflected in its use as one of the Widecombe church bosses.

Two winged heads particularly stand out as being of superior craftsmanship to the others. They are among the bosses at the back part of the church where the roof had to be raised when the tower was built. The Ward Lock guidebook of 1898 says that two bosses in the church represent Henry VIII and Jane Seymour - an unlikely claim for these two?

Leaves and flower motifs are common and include the red rose of Lancashire; the white rose of Yorkshire is also representative of the Virgin Mary. The badge of Henry IV (1461-1483) is a combination of both red and white roses.

At Chittleford a lintel over the fireplace depicts the legend of the fox and the goose, the fox representing the devil and the goose the gullible creature, open to temptation.

THE PULPIT

The Dymond Diaries record that:

'Sunday April 30th (1876) was a great day at Widecombe as the Archdeacon of Totnes came over to spend the day so that the new pulpit might be first preached from by a dignitary of the church.

The Church restoration for which we had all been so anxious and for which all have worked so hard is now completed and as far as it goes is very satisfactory... the old square pews or sleeping boxes have been removed and open seats put in their place. The tower has been thrown into the nave so the church looks larger than ever - and most of the plaster has been scraped away leaving the granite walls exposed - various revelations have been made by the scraping process, the staircase leading to the rood loft, and the curious, and in this part of the world almost unknown, red stone around the niches (or mensa) for the bread and wine in the chancel.

The handsomely carved and extremely massive granite pulpit, the gift of Mr Tucker of Natsworthy, also looks exceedingly well and is suitable in this granite country.'

The Dymonds' initial view was that the pulpit was 'too large'. Possibly its size and height was in keeping with the earlier box pews. It is unclear who made the pulpit. Hermon French writing to the author's mother refers to John L. Webber, the village constable, and says: 'Squire Tucker of Natsworthy presented the granite pulpit to Widecombe church. It was made of granite hewn from boulders on Hamildon'.

Tom Nosworthy pointed out to Hermon French the source of the granite, and he had it from William Warren. Both were masons. It lay on the east slope of Womabarrow in Widecombe Manor and one can still find remains of rejected material and jumper holes in the rock there.

The coat of arms shown in the photograph below are of the Tucker family of Throwleigh and of North Tawton in Devon. It is possible that this stone was originally intended for inclusion in the pulpit but for some reason it was discarded.

John Somers Cocks noted that the had been removed to Newton Abbot at some point before being returned to Widecombe. In a letter to the author's mother he traces the origins of the family from the seventeenth century down to W.V. Owen Tucker who, by 1870, had become Lord of the Manor of Natsworthy.

The stone now rests at the back of a cupboard in the Church House.

The stone bearing the arms of the Tucker family.

The pulpit, carved from stone taken from Hameldown.

ST CATHERINE'S CHAPEL

In December 1966 the vicar reported: 'This month also sees the Dedication of the new Chapel in Widecombe Church. We have so far been calling it the Lady Chapel but I am assured by Mr H. French that it has already been dedicated to St Catherine. This is proved by the fact that records say that a priest asked for burial by this chapel near to his wife [mother?] in the Middle Ages. His tomb is marked by a chalice.'

Hermon French wrote: 'The priest in question was John Shillingford, Canon of Exeter and Rector of Ugborough and Shillingford St George, one of the North Hall family. His will was proved on 16th Oct. 1406.'

The 'new' chapel was part of the restoration programme carried out in the 1960s. The original Lady Chapel would have been in the corresponding part of the church on the north side of the chancel. That there was a chapel of Our Lady in Widecombe can be deduced from the following considerations: since it was usual to dedicate the first chapel consecrated in a church to the Virgin Mary, the existence in Widecombe church of a chapel dedicated to St Catherine suggests a Lady Chapel already existed there. Furthermore since, in medieval times, the position of this chapel was always on the right-hand side of the priest as he faced the congregation, we know where to look for it. In fact we see a very fine stained glass window facing east on the north side of the chancel at Widecombe, the larger central panel being a full-length image of the Virgin. In fact the window is a modern one, dedicated in 1886 to the memory of another Mary, Mary Firth, and replacing a much older window that was in a fragmentary state.

As the Dymond Diaries record, St Catherine's Chapel is one of the few in the country to contain a mensa in a good state of preservation.

St Catherine's Chapel

Above: the likely gravestone of John Shillingford (1406), outside St Catherine's Chapel, inscribed with a chalice.

Left: the mensa in St Catherine's Chapel.

CHURCH AND CHAPEL MUSIC AND GALLERY BANDS

One of the earliest records of Widecombe's west gallery, or singing loft, comes from Polwhele. Describing Widecombe church in 1796 he wrote: 'from altar-piece to singing loft, more than 80 feet.'

With the chancel and nave being 104 feet this would put the choir stalls in front of the great arch. A survey in 1815 shows a plan of the church with the singing loft blocking by the archway of the tower. It also shows the entire interior was filled with box pews. The rood screen had already been removed and the newell staircase blocked off. There was however an exterior door to the chancel, since filled in, although the door and frame outside are still visible.

The following account of church music is provided by Rollo Woods, a notable authority on the subject.

The origins of west gallery music goes back to the Reformation when the *Book of Psalms* was sung to simple, popular tunes. Music in church was frowned on by the Puritans who, by 1644, had destroyed most church organs. After this, singing in church was unaccompanied until the religious revival inspired by the Wesleys affected the musical life of many churches. Choirs came together to practice hymns and psalms and they recruited local musicians to accompany them.

Galleries or platforms were built at the west end of churches and meeting houses to accommodate bands and singers. Between about 1750 and 1800 hundreds of west gallery bands were formed.

Most of the bands performed secular music too, leading village processsions at Whitsun, and playing at social occasions such as harvest festivals and at Christmas.

Churches and chapels supported their bands, buying and maintaining instruments, hiring singing teachers and purchasing song books. Such expenses are noted in churchwarden's accounts.

The west gallery tradition was eventually destroyed by the Victorian clergy, influenced by the Oxford movement. They not only pulled down the galleries but replaced the band with a harmonium or organ. Neglect over the past hundred years has completed what they began..

The main sources of information concerning west gallery bands are: the surviving instruments, the church or chapel records, music books used in the gallery and, more rarely, reports in the local press, travellers' tales and local diaries. Of Widecombe only a few anecdotal memories remain of the Dunstone band, but other sources are well represented.

Churchwardens' accounts and music books confirm that the parish church band consisted of two violins, a flute and a cello. Watergate Baptist chapel had the same combination, while the last band at Dunstone Methodist chapel was a trio, lacking the flute.

Two fiddles, one from the parish church and one from Watergate are thought to survive, also a four-key flute (possible the 'flut' for which the church paid £1.11.6 in 1813). There may be a cello somewhere in the parish - an instrument Hermon French, like Thomas Hardy, called a bass viol.

Eighteenth century account books refer to costs for instruments, 'singing seats' and the singers' platforms and in the early nineteenth century monies were paid to musicians themselves and for the instruction of the choir.

The surviving music books are a wonderful source of information and there are no fewer than seventeen manuscripts and three printed books from Widecombe. They, together with the general church and parish records comprise a priceless legacy of musical history within the parish that continues down to modern times.

A page from one of the Widecombe manuscript music books showing 'The Cottage March' written by Richard French c. 1870.

CHURCH BELLS AND BELL-RINGING

Climbing from the bell loft to the lead roof one is reminded of Dymond's words: 'It is scarcely possible to conceive a position more advantageous than the lofty tower in the vale of Widecombe for the music of church bells.'

There is a peal of six bells, each bearing an inscription: 1. Hear Me When I call; 2. Attend O Ye People; 3. Robeart Hamlyn, Sonne of John Hamlyn, Chittleford T.P. 1632, Gathered of the Young Men and Maid Fyfteen Pounds; 4. Mr John Hext and Mr George Leaman Ch. Wardens, Thomas Bilbie Fecit 1774; 5. Soli Deo Deter T.P. 1663; 6. Draw Near Unto God and God Will Draw Near Unto You T.P. 1632.

The tradition of bell ringing is very much in the parish blood although when it began is not known. Jack Prouse writes: 'Widecombe has for many years maintained a good team of bellringers. Their successes in various competitions can be seen from the certificates on the wall inside the tower door. Miss Penn-Gaskell, who used to live at Scobitor, was very fond of bellringing and gave a trophy for a competition... I was one of the ringers from 1935 until the war (when all bell ringing was banned). There were six ringers in a team who rang for 15 minutes a peal known as 66 on thirds. Violet Warren tells me the first competition was c. 1930 but no records were kept.'

In 1947 there were two teams: Bill Miners, Ern Pascoe, Jeff Hannaford, Frank Dowrich, Reg Norrish, Les Edworthy or Ned Northmore were one team. The other team was Ern Pascoe, Herbert Pascoe, Gerald Lamb, Ned Morthmore, Les Edworthy and Bill Miners. That they were very dedicated can be seen from the story of Les Edworthy whose trousers fell down on one occasion but he gallantly continued ringing until the peal had been completed.

The Bill Miners' Rose Bowl is competed for all over Devon and, following the death of Les Edworthy, an additional cup was given by his wife for the runners-up.

Hand-bell ringing has also had its day in Widecombe for the author's mother organised two teams who would perform for the entertainment of others - and themselves!

Widecombe bell-ringers in the late 1960s. (l-r) W.F. Miners (Bill), Ernest Pascoe (Ern), Gerald Lamb, Joe Addison, Herbert Pascoe (Pickles), Simon Northmore (Ned).

THE CHURCHYARD, BURIALS AND MEMORIALS

The first rector of Widecombe was recorded in 1253 and it is safe to assume that from that date the area around the church was a communal graveyard, even though records of burials go back only to 1560.

From the records it is known that 4044 interments took place between 1560 and 1801, and several hundred burials in the three hundred years before that. Around the churchyard there is a wall five feet high in places with earth reaching to its top. It may well be that when the church was built, and again when the tower was constructed, the foundation soil was spread over earlier burials. The sunken paths and the steps down to the floor of the church are evidence of this. Even so, the ground available for interments must have been re-used several times.

The old practice of burial was to wrap the body in five yards of woollen shroud; it did not become commonplace to erect a headstone until after 1838.

In earlier times parishioners who died would be carried to their burial in Widecombe. The dead from Dartmeet, Hexworthy and other places in that direction would have to be carried up the steep slope of Yar Tor Hill and the bearers would rest at the rock now called the Coffin Stone. Rude stone crosses and the initials of the deceased are carved here.

Another stone bearing a more recent cross is to be found in the base of a wall on Lake Steep, the hill above Poundsgate. This marks the place where a doctor, then living at Beacon Cottage beside the Tavistock Inn, died suddenly while out walking sometime at the turn of the century.

At various other points on the moor memorials have been raised to the dead of the parish. One such is the cross raised in memory of Evelyn Anthony Cave-Penny, killed by a sniper in Palestine on 8 June 1918. It stands atop a small outcrop on the road to Sherill and is inscribed 'Look up and lift your heads.'

Burials inside the church would have been restricted, yet betwen 1712 and 1762 there were sixty-nine such interments. One such was 'Richard Langeworthye of Lyswill, Gent.' who was buried on 17 July 1617 under a stone bearing the epitaph:

The man whose Bodye
Here doth lye
Began to Live
When he did dye
Good both in life
And death he proved
And was of God
And man beloved
Now he lyveth
In haven's joy
And never more
To feel annoye

There are only 277 memorials to be found in Widecombe churchyard, a number of which have been removed from their original location. Many are ascribed to more than one family. With the churchyard considered full, a new area has been brought into use - part of the Sentry (sanctuary) field.

Just after the Great War a new water supply was brought into the church and there are still some people who remember skulls placed on windowsills while excavations took place. It was at this time that a skeleton was unearthed of a man over seven feet in height. The vicar was sent for to view this marvel but the bones turned to dust before he arrived.

In certain circumstances a death in the parish required time-honoured formalities to be undertaken. The churchwardens' accounts for 1747 record 'the account of our Disbursement concerning John Weeks, a man that was drowned in the West Dart and found to ye charges of our P'sh.'

This account reveals that four men watched the body through the first night, three on the following night and two men for a further two nights. The coroner was called from Lydford for he was charged to investigate any death by misadventure or murder with the Forest of Dartmoor.

THE CATHEDRAL OF THE MOOR

Above: Widecombe church cross, discovered in the east wall of the churchyard.

Above left: a view across the churchyard. In the foreground is the gravestone of Olive Katharine Parr, the author Beatrice Chase.

Above left: part of the coffin stone.

Above: the memorial cross to Anthony Cave-Penny.

Below: an incised cross on Lake Steep commemorating the death of a doctor near this point.

Above: the oldest dated gravestone in Widecombe churchyard, 1672.

MARY AND JOHN ELFORD

This memorial, placed on the wall of the north aisle, previously hung in the chancel where it was erected in 1650. It bears an intriguing inscription in memory of Mary Elford, third wife of John Elford of Sheepstor.

The Elfords were an old and well-established family who inhabited a number of Dartmoor's hamlets. John Elford was a prominent citizen who represented Tiverton in the Long Parliament (1640-60), a turbulent period in history. Elford married four times and the monument carries the arms associated with each marriage.

Desperate for a son-and-heir Elford's first three marriages provided him only with daughters and it was his fourth wife, Sarah Wollocombe who eventually provided him with five sons and a daughter.

In common with the fashion of the times, Mary Elford's memorial contains cryptic messages which appear as anagrams and chronograms (the latter using numbers to create words or dates coincident with the life of the deceased).

It is also interesting to speculate as to the reason Mary came to Widecombe for the birth of her children. It is possible that John Elford's royalist sympathies required him to lie low for a while, and where better than in Widecombe where he had family and friends. There are twenty-four entries relating to Elford or Ilford family members in the parish records between 1635 and 1719.

THE CHURCH HOUSE

Church Houses have existed since the twelfth century as places used for parish festivities and church ales. Such festivities did not always enhance the reputation of these buildings to which the following extracts, fortunately not from Widecombe, will testify: 'Hath not the Divell hys chapell close adjoining to God's church?' (1593); and 'As like a church and an ale house, God and the divell they manie times dwell near together.' (1696).

The present structure at Widecombe was built about 1538 and very likely replaced another building. The first recording, in 1608, refers to the lease to John Baker for a one year rent of 24/- for the Church House and the utensils for brewing. The lease stipulated that the utensils had to be returned at the end of the year in the same condition as received. The parishioners retained the right to use the building 'as they had been accustomed.'

The Widecombe Church House has two floors, the upper floors originally being reached by external stairs which have now been blocked off. It also has a penthouse, the 'pentice', a covered way on the opposite side of the stairs. For a great many years the village stocks were kept under the east end of the pentice - showing signs of deterioration they have now been removed.

There are early photographs which show the roof under thatch; the date is not known when it became slate-roofed. The windows are generally small. At nearby Bridford the Revd Carrington described similar openings 'massive with timber, not more than 4 inches between the mullions, and never meant to be glazed, and equally calculated to exclude light.' As Bridford is at about the same height above sea level the same 'unfortunate poor must have suffered much from the winter cold.'

Writing a century before, in 1732, the churchwardens at Widecombe were alive to the situation: 'Pd. for new glazing the under part of the window of the parish house which was enlarged for the Benefit of more light to the house 1/4.'

In 1636 there appears to have been a charity which included the Church House. Certainly in 1810 it was used as a poor house and at other times the Overseers of the Poor used the building as an alms house.

A study of the interior discloses numerous fireplaces indicating that it had previously been subdivided. This is supported by agreements drawn up on 6 May, 1805 in which John Tremills jnr is to have 'the little kitching Chamber, Little Fore Chamber and the School Chamber... and the Linhay in the Back Court for the sum of £2 per year.'

Richard Brooking on behalf of Ann Smerdon got the 'Parlour of the Church House and a little Room Adjoining and part of the Woodhouse for £2 per year.'

On 19 March, 1824, John Potter who, the Vestry proceedings record, was elected to the office of Sexton 'made an application for a house - the meeting resolve that Bet and Mary Leaman shall have lodging in the room adjoining that occupied by their Father and Mother - and that John Potter, his wife and family shall come into the Middle house with Ann Potter and Bet Middleton.'

In the 1861 census the following residences are listed: the Vicarage, Town Mills, Smithhill, Old Inn, Widecombe Village (2), Church House (8), Southcombe Villa and New Park.

From this it will be seen that the Church House was very crowded and that many people had to share rooms.

In 1881 the Church House was sold to the School Board for £220 and was used as such until a new County School was built in the Smooth Meadow part of Southcombe's land, opposite the present Fair field. When renovations to the church took place in 1875 the Church House was used temporarily.

In 1872, Harvest Festival celebrations were held there following the church service: 'everyone retired to the School Room where tea drinking began in earnest... About 200 people each taking about 4 cups of tea each and cake and bread and butter to match kept all hands pretty busy till past 6 o'clock. The evening's entertainment consisting of various songs and glees by Misses Floud and the Ashburton choir and readings by Mr Williams, Mr Jackson and Mr Floud began and seemed to give great satisfaction to the people who crowded the room. The days doings ended by singing "God Save the Queen" about 9.30 and after a vote of thanks our party of six accompanied by Mrs Hannaford and Louisa Jane came home through the muddy roads by lantern light...'

In 1932 the vicar, the Revd E.C. Wood, hearing that the Church House was to be sold, bought it for £1200 with funds he raised himself. In 1933 he presented it to the National Trust, fearing that it might otherwise become a shop or a restaurant. Indeed the National Trust have themselves opened a shop and information office in that part known as the Sexton's Cottage, whilst the remainder is leased back to the parishioners - thus echoing the terms of the John Baker's lease back in 1608.

WIDECOMBE

Above: the Church House today and (**left**) the same scene in the early 1900s when the roof was thatched. The wall in the foreground disappeared for many years but was recently rebuilt by the Dartmoor National Park Authority.

The old stocks once stood beside the entrance to Church House

OTHER PLACES OF WORSHIP

Widecombe church was not the only place of worship in the parish; past documentation tells us that there was a medieval chapel of St Leonard at Spitchwick and, later, chapels at Jordan, Cator and Blackaton. All these may have been built under the benevolence of the local landowner, as was the Catholic chapel at Venton which flourished in the first half of the present century - built by the Parrs.

A study of field names helps to pinpoint where some of these chapels were sited. Great and Little Chapple Park on Spitchwick land suggest the location of St Leonards chapel. The late Edith French who was born and brought up at Spitchwick recalled pieces of masonry lying at the edge of one of these field during her youth. The deacon or minister of the chapel lived at Christian Hays (Lower Town) where a house, once the residence of the Cleave family, is now called Cresson Hays.

Chapel field on Dockwell abuts Watergate Chapel and was probably given its name after the chapel was built. This would not be the case for Chapel Park on great Dunstone as the field next door was and is still known as Lady Meadow. The next field along is Chapel Field which got its name after the Methodist chapel was built, previously known as Willow Piece.

Lady Meadow, appearing under this name for centuries in parish accounts, was a much sought after piece of land, a local farmer describing it as the most fertile field in the parish. To one side stood the original parish cottages. Following the Napoleonic Wars there must have been an upsurge in non-conformist faiths for we find two Methodist chapels, Dunstone and Poundsgate, and a Congregational or Calvanist Chapel at Watergate.

This latter chapel was built in 1834 and survived until 1939. The Revd Leonard J. McCrea, the author's grandfather, a retired Congregational minister, preached there on occasion and the author can remember going there to clear up rubbish just before the beginning of the Second World War,

The two other chapels were built by Weslyan Methodists. Roger Thorne describes that chapels are grouped in 'circuits' with one or more resident ministers, each of whom has 'pastoral charge' of a particular congregation. He suggests 'the genius of Methodism is the circuit principle in which small congregations can survive through being associated with others in a group.'

A guest at Blackslade on 3 September 1872 recalls a chapel service there: 'attending the Dunstone Chapel where I heard a rather illiterate but sound and pithy sermon from one of the "great guns" amongst our chapel-going neighbours.' And again on 15 October: 'managed to walk over to Watergate Chapel to a preaching.' The author too remembers sitting enthralled at Dunstone listening as the minister, often a farmer, haranguing the half dozen faithful.

In a letter to the author Jack Prouse recalls: 'The local preachers usually found their own way by their own transport, motor cycle, bicycle etc. to Dunstone or came by car (usually from Ashburton or Buckfastleigh) which conveyed them to Poundsgate, Dunstone and on to Ilsington. I remember one person, Herbert French, who used to bicycle from South Brent to Dunstone for the 3pm service, have tea either at my grandmother's or at some other chapel lady's house (they had a rota!), take the 6pm service then cycle home. Such was their dedication. Wonderful really.'

Attendances were usually small but that did not matter. Poundsgate was opened in 1854 though there was a lease for the building in 1833.

The membership numbers were as follows: 1885 - 5; 1860 - 6; 1880 - 3; 1900 - 10; 1920 - 12; 1930 -15 and 1940 - 7. Dunstone, built in 1833, has slightly higher membership during this period but never more than 19 members: 1853 - 7; 1860 -19; 1870 - 15; 1880 - 15; 1890 - 11; 1900 - 11; 1910 - 18 and 1920 - 14.

The Dymond diaries record on 27 August 1871: 'Carrie went to Dunstone chapel in the evening and was much edified by the singing which is accompanied by a violin and a flute.' During the author's time hymns were accompanied by the organ played by Lily Hambley for many years, and also by his mother. Sunday School was attended by a host of young people, including the Miners family and the Browns, and the author's grandfather composed special pieces for the choir.

Mrs Kernick, widow of the Widecombe blacksmith gets a special mention in the chapel minutes for having completed fifty years' service.

In more recent years the Moorland Team Ministry came into being the aim of which was to help provide mutual support among ministers who covered several Dartmoor Parishes. In the 1970s the Revd John Brown's responsibilities included the chaplaincy of Dartmoor Prison.

WIDECOMBE

Harvest Festival tea at Watergate Chapel c.1900. *(Gwen Beard)*.

Dunstone Weslyan Church in the 1930s. The four ladies include Annie Hern, Lillian Warren (née Gough), and Alice Hambley (née Warren); the identity of the person on the extreme left is unknown. Note the double doors to the stable at the rear of the church.

OTHER PLACES OF WORSHIP

The interior of Dunstone Methodist Church following restorations in the early 1920s - from a postcard by Chapman & Son. *(Jack Prouse)*.

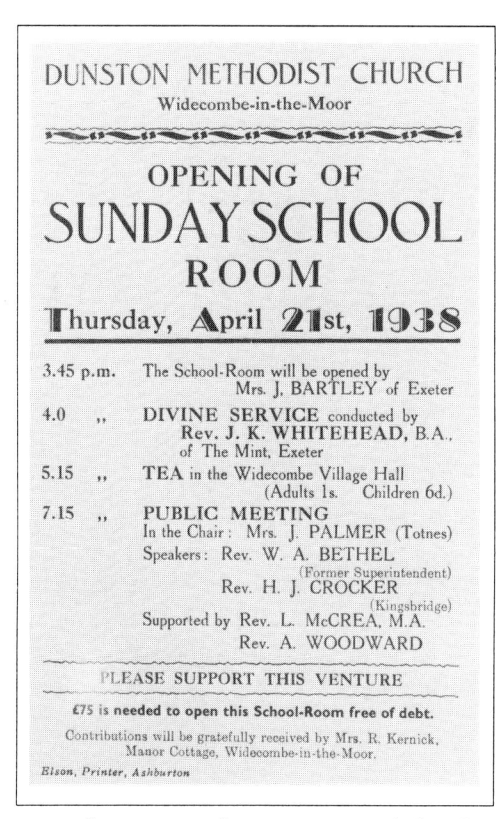

A poster advertising the opening of the Sunday School room in 1938. This was converted from the stable.

Daffodil Walters and Granny Townsend at Brooklands c. 1940. Daffodil was to become a Sunday School teacher at Dunstone. *(Jack Prouse)*.

WIDECOMBE

Dunstone Chapel centenary celebrations, 1933. *(Iris Woods and May Hambley).*

1. Mrs Kernick. *2.* Annie Nosworthy (Stephens). *3.* Mary Kernick. *4.* Mrs Alice Warren. *5.* Louie Caunter (Hannaford). *6.* George Hambley.

Dunstone Chapel Sunday School 1939-40. **Back row (l-r):** Julia Hambley (Morley); Joan Miners (Reddaway); Pam Griver; unknown; unknown; Margaret Miners (Whiteway); Joyce Miners (Ewen); Myra Miners (Lloyd); Phyllis Brown (Pascoe); Edna Brown (Harvey); Bernard Miners; Anthony Brown. **Front row (l-r):** Johnny Basire; Jean Nosworthy; unknown; unknown; unknown; unknown; unknown; Dorothy Brown (Taylor); unknown; John Miners; unknown.

THE CHURCHWARDENS

The inhabitants of Widecombe were fortunate in that they did not live under the rule of a vicar, exercising dictatorial control as would a lord of the manor. The parishioners were able to exert a large degree of self control and this they achieved under a system of local government which had its roots in common law.

By and large the parishioners had to carry out compulsory duties for the good of all under the direction of the wardens. This office was itself very demanding, took a great deal of time, and was unpaid. It was an unpopular role and this is possibly one reason why each person held the post for only one year.

To ease the burden the parish was divided into four quarters with the number of officers appropriately proportioned: two churchwardens, four overseers of the poor, four highway surveyors and a constable.

The four quarters of the parish were: Coombe (Natsworthy and Widecombe Town Manors, with Dunstone and Blackslade Manors); Dewdon (with Blagdon Pippard or Blackaton); Spitchwick; and the Ancient Tenements which formed the Forest Quarter.

An old parchment preserved at Widecombe lists the tenements from which churchwardens were drawn, and often includes the wardens' names: 'John Hexts Huccaby and Elias Smerdon's Norraway; Tunhill and Andrew Hannaford's Hexworthy; Lower Aish and Stephen Townsend Jordan; Andrew Hammets Cator and Higher Bittleford.'

The personal name simply identified the tenement in Huccaby, Norraway (Northway), Jordan and Cator, not necessarily the churchwarden, there being every likelihood that the owner and occupier were different.

The document, possibly rewritten from other lists, was compiled in 1750, for all the entries from 1660-1750 are in the same hand. After 1750 each pair of churchwardens was recorded as they took office. The list ends in 1821 and some years are missing. It is possible that the vicar from that date, Revd James Holman Mason, being autocratic, exercised his right to choose the churchwardens for himself.

Widecombe is fortunate in having a fine set of records and accounts which the wardens kept meticulously. The penmanship is generally excellent and the variations in spelling add charm to these records, for example in the list of tools for roadmending: 1 sledg (1780); 1 sledge (1782); 2 Sloges (1783); 1 Wheelbarrow (1782); 3 whillbarras (1783). A much later entry suggests that 'the undermenshioned children should be anokerlated at the expense of the parish.'

To compliment the documents in the parish chest are the registers of Marriages, Baptisms and Burials, first required by Thomas Cromwell in 1538 during the reign of Henry VIII. Early records are sparse and confusing for the local historian: for instance in 1756 two Joan Hamlyns died but no further details are given. A John Leaman died in 1748, 1749 and 1754. On 11 October in 1761 John Hamlyn married Grace Stancombe and on 4 November John Hamlyn married Grace Langworthy. The children from such a marriage will appear in the Baptismal Register simply as the son or daughter of John and Grace.

There were twelve main families: Caunter, French, Hamlyn, Hannaford, Hext, Leaman, Mann, Norrish, Nosworthy, Smerdon, Townsend and Willcocks. Only seven still survive. Warren, Cleave and Beard arrived later and are still flourishing. Variations in spelling are rife: Cleave is often spelt Cleve; Leaman as Leyman, etc.

There was a recognisable division of such family names between the upper end of the parish and the lower end. In the lower part the old families were Caunter, Chaffe, Cleave, Easterbrook, French, Hext, Prouse, Turner and Warren. Chaffe and Turner are not found in Widecombe village, Caunter, Cleave and Esterbrook infrequently, but French and Warren are found throughout.

Cecil Torr writes: 'In 1642 the Lords and Commons required returns of all those who, over the age of eighteen, had taken a Protestation against Popery, etc.' The return for Widecombe shows twenty-five named Hamlyn or Hamlin, of these there were six named Richard, four Thomas and three John. No one refused the protest so this document provides an accurate census for the male population aged eighteen and over. The 255 in Widecombe are listed in alphabetical order, each person with a single first name and, again, the same family names appear throughout.

WIDECOMBE

A page from the Churchwardens' accounts of 1761 recounting the curious tale of the farmers who killed a hare.

'Whereas on ye 28th day of January last several Farmers of this Parish went out with the Intention of destroying Foxes, and Accidentally happened to kill an Hair. And whereas Stephen Townsend went to the Justice of the Peace, & informed against them for killing ye sd Hair, & caused ye Penalty of five Pounds to be levied on ye Account, And whereas ye sd Stephen Townsend hath hereforeto received considerable Sums of Mony from ye Parish for killing Foxes, it is unanimously agreed at a Parish meeting called for yt, Purpose, yt, ye said Stephen Townsend shall not be entitled to any Reward from ye Parish for killing of Foxes, till he hath brought in such number as Will make up for ye said five Pounds wch, he hath caused to be levied by these his vexatious Proceedings...'

The document indicates the power wielded by churchwardens through local meetings, and also demonstrates the natural justice which the people of Widecombe were able to carry out on one who had clearly overstepped the bounds of propriety as far as his fellow parishioners were concerned. The vicar and twenty-eight parishioners have signed the document.

Churchwardens' names imprinted on the lead roof of the church in 1749.

OVERSEERS OF THE POOR

The overseers of the poor had a very onerous job, responsible as they were for the poor when a labourer's wage provided little above subsistence. Those destitute could receive money from the poor rate, materials from the parish chest and, very occasionally, food.

Illegitimate children were a heavy burden, the father being automatically made to assume responsibility for his children, otherwise the parish in which the child was born had to bear the expense. The overseers kept a watchful eye on such expectant arrivals: In 1723 the records relate: 'warrant for Richard Hodge of Ashburton to appear before Justice Boyan to give account of what parish he belongeth to 6d. And for a warrant to apprehend his wife for intruding herself into our parish as an inmate and was like to have child in our parish and be chargeable here 6d.'

It rested with the mother to name the father of her child and it was not uncommon for unmarried mothers to be carried over the boundary just before childbirth to avoid the burden falling on the parish. Although this unsavoury practice was not followed in Widecombe the overseers would do their duty to ensure that the offending couple got married. An example is the marriage between John Brooking and Ann Scree in 1755. 'Pd. Richard Smerdon and Saml. White for going to Brixham and apprehending John Bruking and carrying him to Justice and from thence to Widecombe and the next day to Totnes for to have licence...'.

The accounts show various sums relating to this journey included fees for the marriage licence, food and lodging. These costs increased as Brooking failed to turn up in front of the magistrate and a warrant for his arrest was secured. Finally the parish paid for a wedding dress, hat, apron and handkerchief for Ann Scree.

In all the costs came to £11.9.0d., a considerable sum, but obviously thought to be worthwhile in order to rid the parish of Ann Scree, her expectant child and a previous child.

The total expense for burying a pauper also fell on the parish Poor Rate. The costs of Elizabeth Aptor's funeral in 1756 included: 'Pd. Mary Cornish for stretching her forth and affadavit 3/-. Burying suit 4/-. For a coffin 6/6. Making the grave 1/-. Expended at her burial 2/6.'

If the deceased had any property of value it would be sold to defray such costs and any possessions obtained from the parish chest would be returned. In 1728: 'Received for Susan Quint's stockings and shoes 2/-.' The household goods left by her are listed: 'one iron crock, pottcrock and bailer, one little box, two clomen dishes, two spoones, one little clomen pann, one washing tubb, besides a bedstead matt and cords, feather pillow and coverlett.'

The overseers worked hard to find employment for the poor and, in the case of children, apprenticeships would be found. In the 1841 census return of Lizwell, in the ownership of Lady Carew, the occupier was Nicholas Easterbrook (aged 45), his wife (40) and four children. Under the same roof resided: Othnile Baddick (25), labourer; George Leaman (15) apprentice; Robert Smerdon (14) apprentice; Robert Symons (12) ag. labourer; Wm Stancombe (13) apprentice; Henry Pasmore (10) farm servant; Eliz Irish (15) farm servant; and Eliza French (11) farm servant.

A boy's apprenticeship lasted until they were 21, and a girl's until she was 21 or married. They were unpaid.

The overseers could exercise tremendous power with regard to binding out such children of the poor with no reference to family or other authority. They could also command suitable persons to sign indentures.

On 18 April 1823: 'Thos. Rendle's child to be bound an apprentice the overseer is requested to inform him of it. Sam. White's maid to be bound apprentice and the overseer must look to its being done.'

On 22 August 1823: 'The overseer of Combe is to apply to Mr Palk for a summons for Richard Tremain for his Refusal of not sining an Indenture of a poor apprentice.' And 3 October 1823: 'John Hext be desired by Farmer Beard to attend the next vestry meeting in order to produce Indentures that have not been executed and if he fails in doing so the Vestry will feel compelled to summon him before a magistrate.'

The overseers took a dim view when an apprentice absconded or was sent back from the employer to whom he was bound. On 2 April 1824: 'Farmer Beard attended and reported the return of Samuel Robinson late an apprentice at Lower Torr who was sent back from Devonport with an order and Mr Mason is desired to write to Mr Palk to Bind him out on one of those farmers who had taken parish apprentices with a premium from Devonport or any other place.'

The overseers received and distributed monies bequeathed to the parish, charitable bequests, and

Pages from the account book for the Overseers of the Poor for November and December 1765.

fines that had been collected by the Constable (1719: 'Rec'd of John Stitson 2/- being convicted of prophane swearing of an oath.').

It might seem desirable for a parish not to have the burden of any 'poor' but we read in the Revd Carrington's *Parochiales Bridfordii* that 'one aged villager told the Rector that he remembered when Bridford parish forced half-a-crown weekly upon an old cottager because they had not chargeable poor, and the Act of Elizabeth provided that, where a parish had not poor of its own, it should be united to the next parish where poor were chargeable.'

In the mid nineteenth century many parishes in England subscribed to a Union Workhouse where the poor were forced to live and work often in appalling condition. The Church House was retained for this purpose in Widecombe and the parishioners defied pressure to send the poor of the parish into such penury. Indeed throughout the accounts it is clear that, bad though conditions might be for those in poverty, the overseers in Widecombe strived hard to ensure that, although the harsh Poor Laws was properly upheld, that the plight of those in need should not be worsened by pitiless action.

JANE SMERDON WIDECOMBE APPRENTICE

The overseers' records and other parish registers provide the researcher not simply with a list of names and dates, but with an insight into the lives of ordinary families and individuals from the past.

For instance the Burial Register reveals that Joan Smerdon (widow) and two of her children Joan and Mary died in May 1768. The overseers duly sold the property and goods belonging to the deceased: 'Received for Joan Smerdon's goods £3.15.10d'; and 'Received of George Layman £10.12.6d for Joan Smerdon's share of Combe' and from this they deducted the costs of the burials.

John Smerdon, Joan's husband, had died the previous year leaving his widow and children to the mercy of the family and parish. The Baptism Register reveals that Joan and John Smerdon had four children, two of which, Jane and John, were now orphaned.

Further searches of the records provide a fascinating glimpse of how the parish looked after its own in the case of this family.

It is clear that food and nursing care was provided during the period of illness that brought about the death of Joan and two of her children. 'Pd. Ely. Ruby for attendance about Joan Smerdon' and that Jane Leamon, sister-in-law to Joan, and her husband George Leaman undertook to house and clothe the widow and her family. 'Pd. Jane Leaman for Joan Smerdon's children 5/6. Paid Jane Leaman for knitting two pairs of stocking and making 2 shirts and other things 1/6.'

A year later, in 1769, when John was aged 3 and his sister 8, Jane Smerdon was taken by her aunt Jane Leaman to be apprenticed in Newton Abbot: 'Pd. for Jane Leaman and the child to ride to Newton and the Turnpick 1/1.' A search of the Indenture records produces the information that Jane was apprenticed to Jacob Ellis, Yeoman of Moretonhampstead, till she reached the age of 21 or married. Being bound as an apprentice outside the parish meant that the people of Widecombe no longer had to share the burden of the costs relating to Jane and she disappears from the parish records. We do know that the young John Smerdon continues in the care of the parish, for 6/- is paid every month for 'the late Joan Smerdon's child.' Then in June 1770 we find: 'Parish funeral for Joan Smerdon's child, grave 1/- coffin 5/-.'

George and Jane Leaman who looked after their relations lived on into the next century. We read in the Burial Register: 'Leaman George, aged 66, 17 June 1802;' and 'Leaman Jane, aged 68, 28 March 1808.'

A page from the account book of the overseers of the poor recording payments made to Joan Smerdon and her children, and assistance given to enable her to claim a right in Combe.

FRIENDLY SOCIETIES

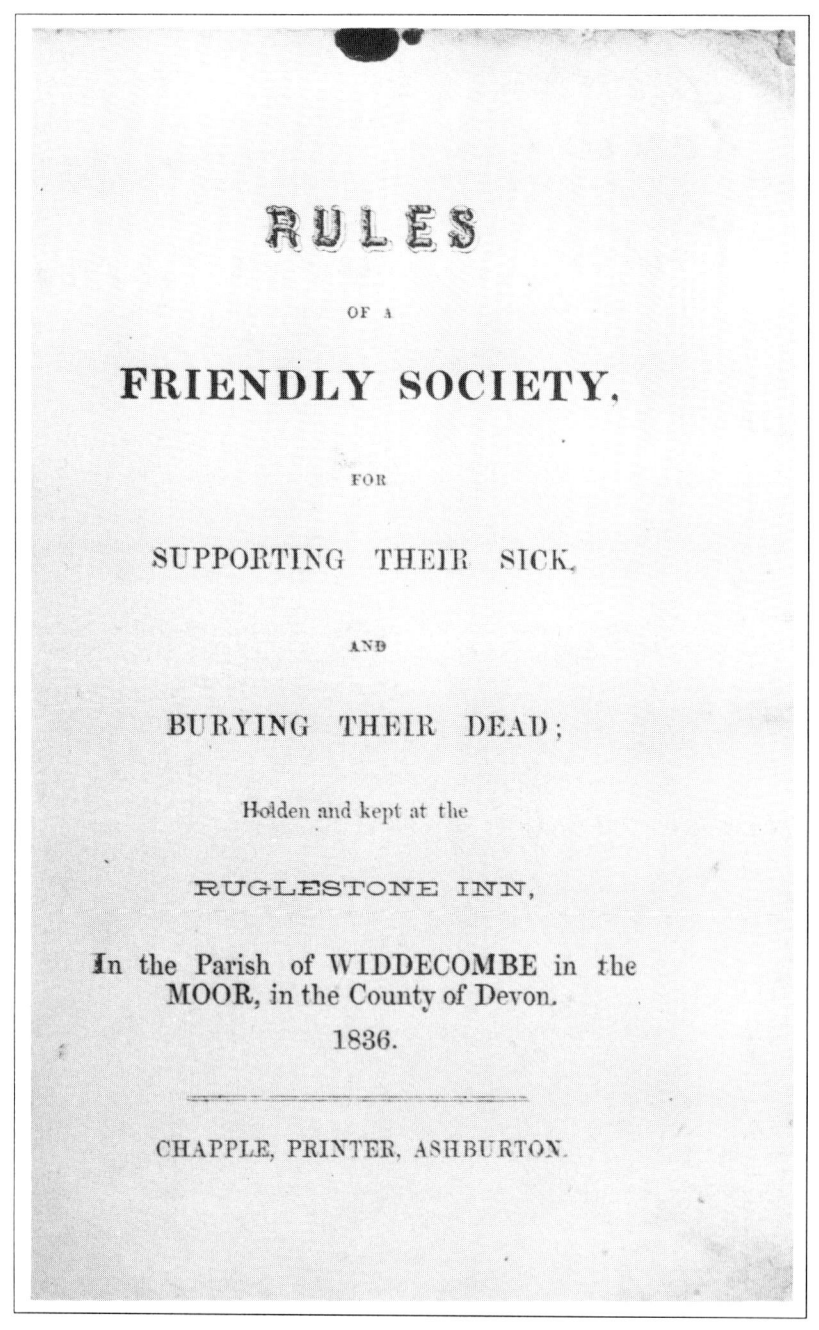

```
RULES
OF A
FRIENDLY SOCIETY,
FOR
SUPPORTING THEIR SICK,
AND
BURYING THEIR DEAD;
Holden and kept at the
RUGLESTONE INN,
In the Parish of WIDDECOMBE in the
MOOR, in the County of Devon.
1836.

CHAPPLE, PRINTER, ASHBURTON.
```

The cover from Louis George Hannaford's Friendly Society rule book recording his entry into the Rugglestone 'club' on 15 September 1902. *(Deborah Hannaford).*

Though the Overseers of the Poor provided help for those in extreme circumstances, from the 1830s onwards those parishioners who were able to afford it began to join insurance associations to support them in time of need. One such Friendly Society was based at the Rugglestone Inn and a page from its Rule Book, dated 1836, is shown opposite.

Louis George Hannaford joined the society in 1902. The enrolment fee was 2/6d plus 6d for a copy of the rules. The quarterly dues were 2/3d which also entitled the member to a free pint of beer. The records and monies were kept in a box with three locks and keys for security and when the sum accrued reached £200 it was used to pay members' fees. The balance of funds was never allowed to fall below £30.

One rule was clearly designed to perpetuate the society: 'any member proposing its (the society's) dissolution shall forfeit five shillings.' Another reflects modern private health care insurance and shows that things have changed little over the years: 'That no person shall be admitted into the society who has any old grief or malady.'

The compensation due to members was 'That if any member, after being a payer for one year, shall be afflicted by the hand of God with any sickness or bodily hurt, and not through any wilful act or cause of his own, he shall receive eight shillings per week if confined to bed.'

'Walking pay' was four shillings per week, equivalent to the weekly wage of an agricultural labourer.

The Rugglestone 'club' appears in the Southcombe diaries and the author believes it is still in operation today.

PARISH SCHOOLS

Writing in 1808 Charles Vancouver in his survey of the county epitomised the attitude of the educated classes towards the labourer:

'The peasants mind should never be inspired with a desire to amend his circumstances by the quitting of his cast, but every means the most benevolent and feeling heart can desire, should be employed to make that situation as comfortable and as happy to him as possible, and to which end nothing more essential could contribute, than by exciting a general emulation to excel in all their avocations, even to those of breaking stones for a lime kiln, or for repairing the highways.'

Or as the Reverend Carrington put it, writing a few years later:

In considering the effects of the education system upon the great mass of the population of a country we must not lose sight of the knife and fork philosophy; it may be very well to put a goose quill into the tired hand of a labourer or mechanic after a toilsome day, but I think a goose's drumstick would suit him better. We can exist without the acquisition of much knowledge, but we cannot without eating.'

Thus education for the common people was not held to be desirable either for them or for their supposed 'betters'. Early schooling was part of religious education and, for most children, work on the farm or in service, would be a priority.

When education first began or where it was taught in Widecombe is not known. We do know that Richard Hill, described as 'schoolmaster', signed the Declaration of Conformity on 19 August, 1662, and that (presumably) the same Richard Hill, Literatus, was licenced by the Bishop on 8 June, 1632 to teach English in the parish.

It is known that during the eighteenth century part of the Church House was being used as school, at which time it would have been left to charitable works and the goodwill of individuals to ensure that children received a rudimentary education.

A number of such Charity Schools existed in the parish before the advent of the Board School in 1870. The charity rules were as follows:

1. That no child be admitted to this Charity whose parents can afford to pay for their instruction.
2. That none be admitted under the age of 4 years.
3. That each child be admitted to three years instruction.
4. That each child at his or her dismission from school shall be presented with a bible and some religious book.
5. That the children after their dismission, if within a convenient distance, shall attend the Sunday School and be examined from time to time by the Minister.
6. That this Charity be extended to all poor children, residents in Withycombe or in the Forest of Dartmoor whether belonging to the Parish or not.
7. That there shall be a meeting of Farmers and any other persons who choose to attend in the Parish Chamber on some day every year between the first of March and Easter, when the annual account of the Charity for the past year shall be exhibited.
8. And that this account be afterwards shown to each subscriber and then deposited in the Parish Chest.

There were Charity Schools at Venton, Ponsworthy, Merripit, Hexworthy, Hannaford and Widecombe. Another school existed at Dunstone in 1850 but this may have been 'private'.

The school register at Venton in 1797 lists the following attendees:

Jane Leaman	admitted Feb 1794
William Leaman	admitted June 1795
Elizabeth Potter	admitted Feb 1794
James Leaman	admitted
Sally Leaman	admitted Feb 1796
Sarah Potter	admitted Feb 1794
John Wrayford	admitted
Mary Andrews	admitted Feb 1794
Joseph Leaman	admitted Jan 1796
Susanna Withycombe	admitted Feb 1796
William Thorn	admitted Nov 1796
Thomas Warren	admitted Oct 1796
Caleb Andrews	admitted Jan 1797
Jenny Wrayford	admitted Nov 1797

On Easter Monday, April 17 1797 the children were examined and those having attended for three years were dismissed and were presented with bibles and Watts' *Songs*.

Of those listed above James Leaman died in his youth, Sally Leaman was removed to Widecombe Town school, Mary Andrews was apprenticed to Sylvester Mann and William Thorn was to become a hero at Waterloo.

The Widecombe School Board were always short of money and the teacher's pay was greatly affected by the numbers in attendance.

Leusdon school was founded as a 'mixed school for Boys and Girls, and parents were requested, who wish to send their children, and to pay a penny per week without writing, and two pence per week including writing.'

A succession of female teachers obviously found it difficult to exercise control over the unruly country boys. From the Leusdon school log book we find that Mrs Georgina Jones was dismissed after six months, to be followed by Mrs Emma Elliot Greatwood who caned vigorously (and who died after six months!). Mrs Caroline Elizabeth Cambell lasted three-and-a-half years until she left in December 1884. Her error in marking a boy 'present' when he had died during the previous month was overlooked as being confusion caused by her predecessors.

The next headteacher was a departure from the usual 'Dame', the appointee being Samuel Wills. He lasted three years but was caught keeping two sets of registers, fiddling the books to increase his grant. He went on to make his name with a charitable organisation, also writing several books of poetry.

Joshua Bancroft took over, and though he suffered from bad management and poor pay he stayed on for thirty-three years, retiring in 1921. A number of remarks in the school log illustrate his problems: 'The Board considered I had done wrong in dismissal of scholars when only 12 or 15 were present. In future I must keep school if 10 are present. Of course the master must bear the loss of attendance.'

The appointment of an assistant caused him to observe caustically: 'She asked for a low salary and was therefore accepted. Salary the first consideration here, education and skill second.'

The Widecombe School log survives from 1876 and makes fascinating reading. In that year the reasons given for absences included: 'Dropping potatoes (planting); building a wall; sheep-shearing; and inability to pay fees; digging potatoes.'

Inclement weather forced school closures: 31 January 1881: 'Extra fortnights holiday, severe weather'. December 1882: 'Snow, children unable to cross moor.' Sickness and ill health also brought forced absences from 'bad colds', through whooping cough, mumps, and measles.

School treats were always popular and the Dymond Diaries describe events on 4 July, 1871:

The heavy showers that fell during the morning made us fear that Widecombe School-treat would be a failure, however, at half past one notwithstanding a tremendous shower we set off for Widecombe and reached the church just in time for the service at which about 40 children were present.

The tea was afterwards laid out on the terrace and after some play in the field the children were summoned to their meal. Just then Mr Floud from Ashburton arrived and was very helpful in attending on the little folk and plates of cake and buns disappeared with astounding rapidity. The Firths from Cator arrived just when tea was over and joined in the various games... till nearly 9 o'clock.

Such games they were too. Drop the handkerchief. Mulberry Tree. Cat and Mouse, and all the old set of games of that sort for the girls - seemed the proper thing.

Mr Floud, Miss Firth and Carrie having the chief management of that part of the proceedings had to exercise considerable ingenuity in inventing fresh amusements and at last reached such a pitch that Mr Floud proposed as a last resort 'leap frog' which however was deemed just a little too rough, though the girls were the roughest, some of them.'

At the Board School and later at the County School prizes were awarded for good attendance during the year - a necessary incentive when the demands of a farming community required all hands to help with harvesting. etc.

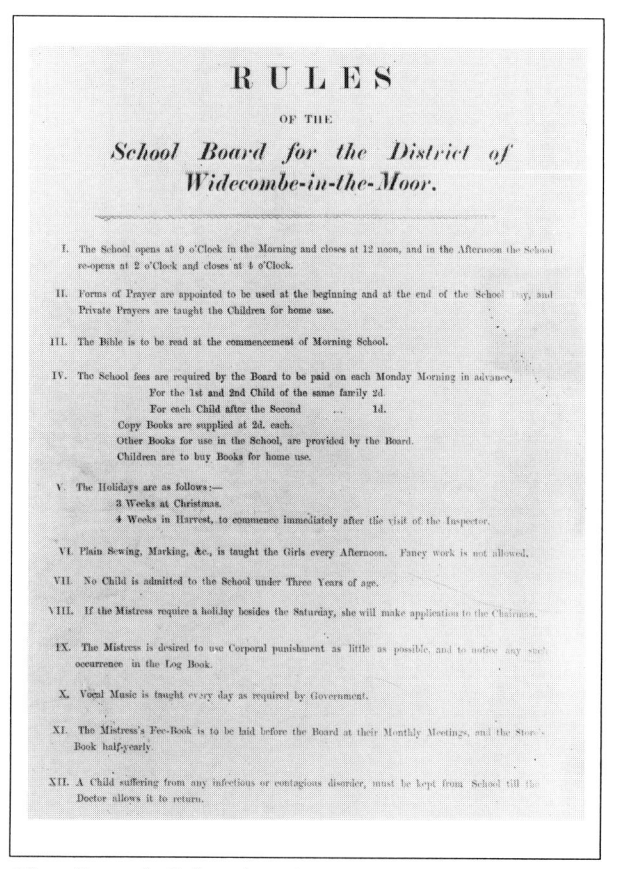

The Board School rules making clear to the 'Mistress' her duties as laid out by the Board governors. *(Iris Woods)*.

PARISH SCHOOLS

Widecombe School girl pupils taken in the early years of the century. They are not in uniform but wear the everyday dress of the times, complete with white pinafores. *(Thirza Nosworthy)*.

Widecombe School c. 1903. Louise, Rosa and Mary Kernick are sitting fourth, fifth and eighth from left in the middle row, with Ethel Kernick on the end. Lily Kernick is tenth from the left in the front row. *(Ena Prowse)*.

WIDECOMBE

Widecombe School girls c. 1907.

Widecombe School boys c. 1907. **Standing (back row l-r)**: Miss Mary Wilcocks; unknown; unknown; unknown; Herbert Hannaford; Bill Bray; John Irish; Mrs Bates; **(middle row l-r)**: Arthur Hern; unknown; Oliver Beard; Bill Miners; Thomas Nosworthy; **(front row)**: George King; unknown; Bert King; Bill Hamlyn; Reg Cole; Andrew Harvey.

PARISH SCHOOLS

School friends, 1912 (l-r): Thirza Irish (Nosworthy); Hilda Beard; Frances Irish; Bessie Beard; Clara Hext; Dorothy Opie. *(Thirza Nosworthy)*.

Widecombe School c. 1930. (**Back row l-r**): Helen Hannaford; Leslie White; Joan Norrish (Phyllis); Harold Cambridge; Miss Brinn (Headmistress); Charlie French; Eleanor French (infant teacher); Gordon Smale; Thirza Caunter (Axford); Evelyn Norrish; (**middle row**): Jack Burgess (standing); Bessie Turner (French); Frank Burgess; Catherine French; Joan Warren (Harvey); Agnes Heywood (Molly - Vincent); Rosemary Hazel; Gladys French; Stanley French (standing); (**front row**): Evelyn Tall; unknown; Margaret Tall; Clifford White; Grace Lane. *(Iris Woods)*.

WIDECOMBE

Widecombe Council School, 1937 (**back row l-r**): Mrs Tucker (teacher); George Germon; Ted Wilcocks; Jean Pearse; Joan Palmer (Hambleton); Deborah Hannaford; May Hambley; Daffodil Walters; Kenneth Pearse; Joyce Brimacombe; (**second row**): Geoffrey Hannaford; Dennis Southcott; Audrey Lamb; Phyllis Brown; Myra Miners; Joan Miners; Stella Brown (Horton); Julia Hambley (Morley); Joyce Miners(?); Fred Germon; (**third row**): Tony Courtier; Francis Germon; Margaret Miners; Dorothy Brown (?); Edna Brown; Dick Brown; Bill Nosworthy (from Shallowford); (**front row**): Bernard Miners; Tony Brown; Tom Nosworthy; Johnny Miners; Ted Hannaford; Bill Nosworthy (from Bonehill). *(May Hambley).*

Empire Day, 1928/29 (l-r): Margaret Nosworthy; Richard Hannaford; Charlie Hannaford; Lydia Hannaford; Raymond Warren; Phyllis French; Dorcas Papworth; Phyllis Papworth; Joyce Brimblecombe (?); Evelyn Daw; Henry Horton; Wilfred Hext; Bob Morley (with union flag); Gilbert Morley (?); Flora Hannaford; Betty Butler (with union flag); Joyce Hine; Jack Prouse (shading eyes); Phyllis Horton (half-hidden); Doreen Hannaford; Roy Hannaford; Richard Horton; unknown; Alec Walters (back, in hat); Anthony Irish (in sash); Violet King; Louise Hannaford; Brian Nosworthy. *(Jack Prouse - 'The one who spoilt the photo - who else!').*

PARISH SCHOOLS

Widecombe School boys outing, 1921 (**back seat l-r**): Jack Irish; Sidney Beard; Norman Nosworthy; Cyril Daw; Ronald Hill; (**second seat**): Raymond Warren; Cyril Warren; Cliff (?) Morley; Kenneth Brown; Revd Coloys Wood; (**third seat**): Charlie Hannaford (half hidden); Dick Hannaford; Alec Walters; Wilfred Hext; Southcott (?); Mr Bates (husband of schoolteacher); (**fourth seat**): Brian Nosworthy; Phyllis French; Linda French (Nosworthy); Fred Daw; Miss Annie Beard (school caretaker); (**front seat**): Mr Hall; driver; Fred Wilcocks; Brown (?); Dennis Nosworthy. *(Iris Woods).*

Widecombe School girls outing, 1921 (**back seat l-r**): Flora Hannaford (Brown); Ruby Hill (Badcock); Mary Cole; Ruth Hannaford (Rowe); Lydia Hannaford (Avery); Dorothy Miners (Parsons); (**second seat**): Margaret Satterly (Dowrick); Mrs Marion Wood (wife of Revd Wood); Rose Hannaford (leaning forward); Leonora (Joan) Irish (French); Thirza Horton (Frost); (**third seat**): Margaret Nosworthy (Harris); Louisa Nosworthy (Irish); Pheobe Wilcocks (Beeble); Vera Hannaford; Stella Nosworthy; (**fourth seat**): Elsie Irish (Hannaford); Evelyn Daw; Joyce Brown; Phyllis Papworth (French); Dorcas Papworth (Steer); (**front seat**): driver; unknown child; Mrs Bates (schoolteacher). *(Iris Woods).*

WIDECOMBE

Widecombe School register of attendance for the school year ending in 1914. The figures show the total number of attendances out of a possible 441. Prizes for attendance were presented - four shillings being awarded for full attendance. *(Hermon French).*

PARISH SCHOOLS

LEUSDON SCHOOL

Above: Leusdon school today.

Below: Schoolchildren at Leusdon c. 1910.

WIDECOMBE

Leusdon school c. 1910. (**Back row l-r**): Joshua Bancroft (schoolmaster); Loisa Caunter; Thirza Cole; Thirza Mann; Bessie Parnell; Annie French; Edith Williams; Mary French; Annie Norrish; Cissie Beard; Florrie Norrish; Blanche Stephens; (**middle row**):Dorothy Hext; Emily Caunter; Blanche Hannaford; Mabel Hannaford; Elsie Nosworthy; L. French; Ethel Ramsey; (**front row**): Doris Townsend; George French (Kimberley); Margery Bancroft; Lily Warren; Florrie French; Alice French; Blanche French; Louise Ramsey; unknown; Rhoda Bancroft; Thirza Norrish; Francis Irish; Winnie Bancroft (standing extreme right). *(Marjorie and Geoff Weymouth)*.

Leusdon Girl Guides, 1911. *(Marjorie and Geoff Weymouth)*.

PARISH SCHOOLS

Leusdon School in the 1900s. The photograph is believed to have been taken a year or so before that on the page facing. (**Back row l-r**): Mrs Prowse; Doris Townsend (Hare); Olive Caunter; Thirza Norrish; unknown; unknown; Laura French; unknown; (**middle row**): Annie Norrish; unknown; unknown; unknown; Blanche Stephens (May); Elsie Nosworthy (Brooks); unknown; Joshua Bancroft (schoolmaster); (**front row**): Florrie French (Veale); Florrie Cleave; Gertie Nosworthy (Norrish); unknown; unknown; Florrie Hamlyn; Blanche French (Oxenham); unknown. *(Iris Woods)*.

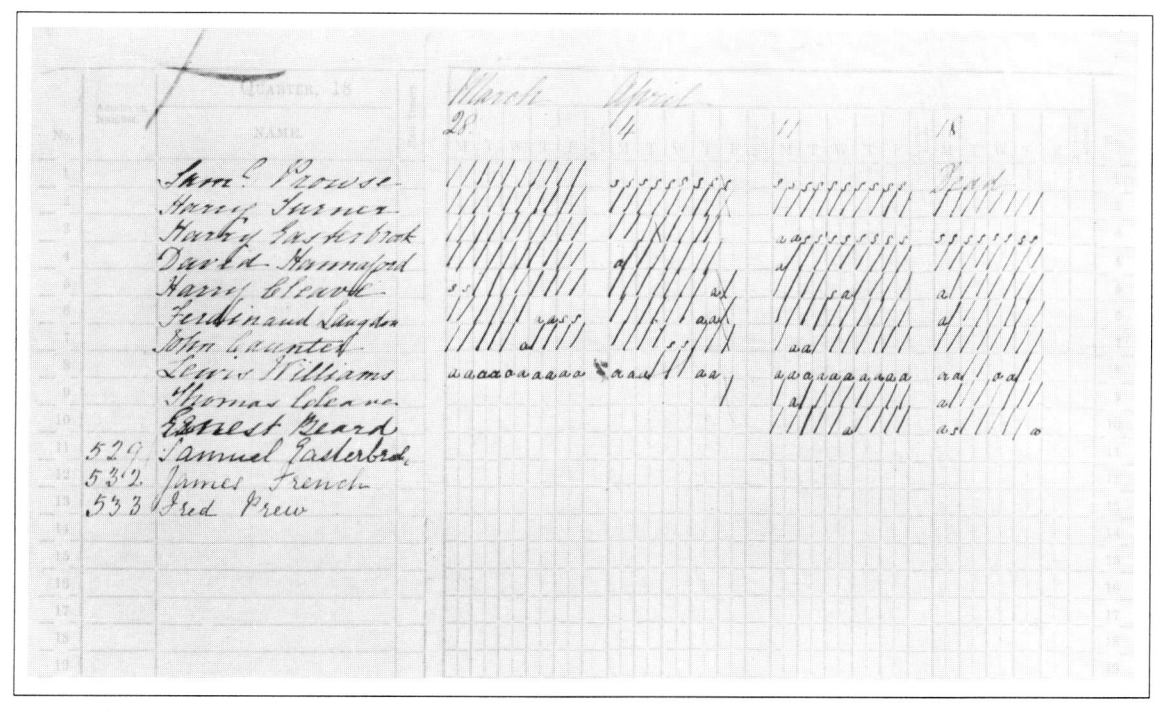

A page from Leusdon school register c. 1900. *(Iris Woods)*.

WIDECOMBE

Attendances at the Leusdon Board School
for year ended June 30th 1899.

400 and over.

8/-	Allen Bancroft	435	I will give 1/6 out of Allen's
3/-	Willie Warren	429	money to Willie Warren, next
3/-	Ella Prowse	427	to him. If Willie had made
3/-	Percy Prowse	423	433 I would have given her
3/-	Leonard Bancroft	411	half of my boy's extra money
3/-	Bertha Hill	400	

Under 400

2/6	George Hambley	399	1/-	Maud French	337
2/6	George Michelmore	392	1/-	Willie Bamsey	336
2/6	Alice Hambley	392	1/-	George Warren	341
2/6	Thomas Bamsey	384	1/-	Ernest Warren	318 left
2/6	Mabel Hill	387	1/-	Hilda Cleave	313
2/6	Edith French	375	1/-	Ellen French	310
1/6	Arthur Caunter	373	1/-	Nancy French	316
1/6	Emmeline French	364	1/-	Willie Michelmore	302
1/6	Jasper French	368	1/-	George Bamsey	300
1/6	John Michelmore	366			
1/6	George Turner	360			
1/6	Herbert Warren	356			
1/6	Jessie Caunter	354			
1/6	Winifred Bancroft	359			
1/6	Louis Warren	357			
1/6	John Bamsey	358			
1/6	John Hannaford	359			

Under 350

1/-	Annie Bamsey	346
1/-	Annie Caunter	337
1/-	Bessie Warren	330
1/-	Annie French	336

A page from Leusdon School register showing attendance for the school year ending in June 1899. Prize money to the value of eight shillings was given to for the highest attendance record. *(Hermon French).*

PARISH SCHOOLS

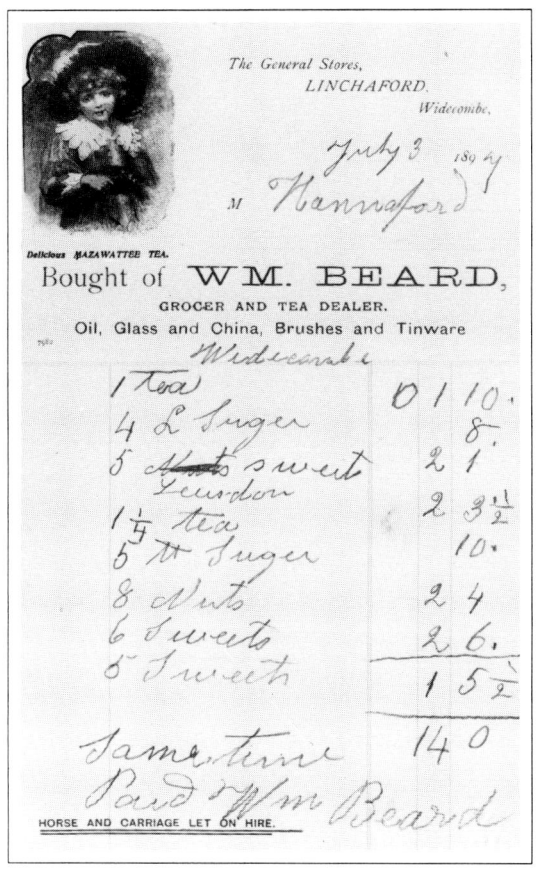

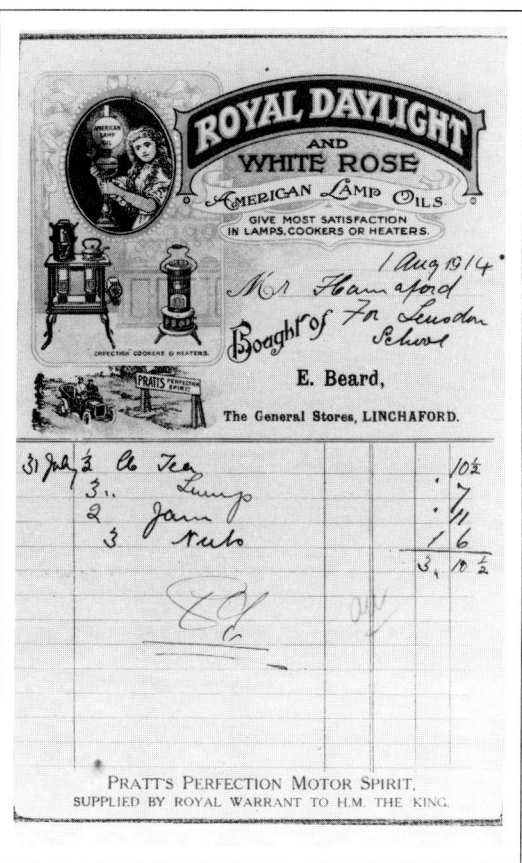

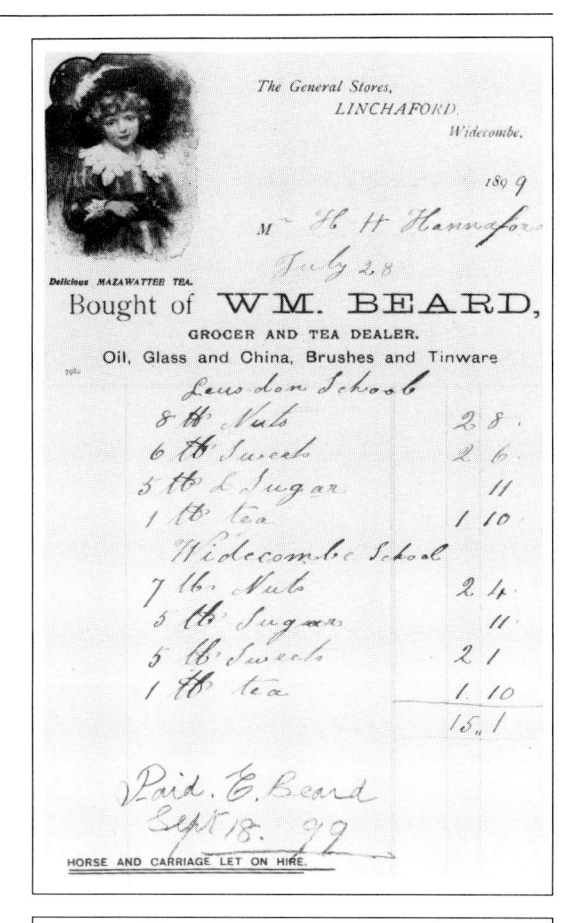

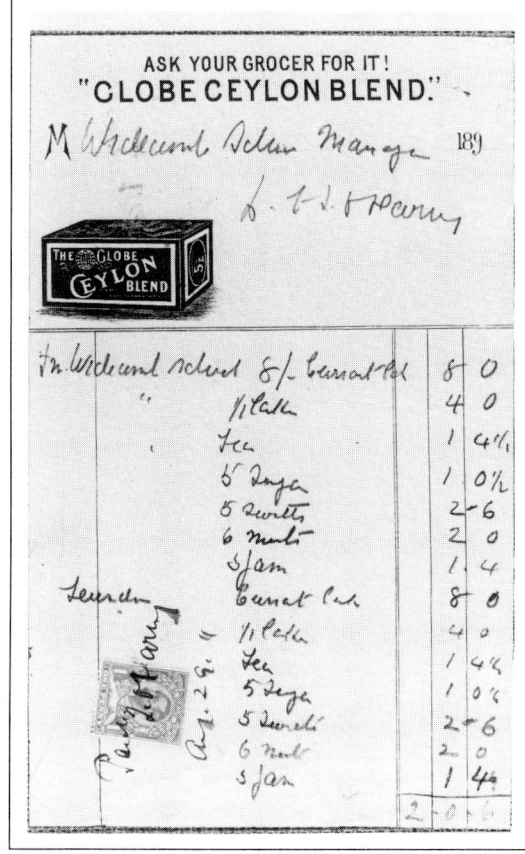

Four bills relating to Widecombe and Leusdon school treats in (clockwise from top left) 1897, 1899, 1911 and 1914. The 1911 bill is from Louis Harvey's shop and post office in the village. *(Hermon French)*.

Fred Walters in the forge c. 1925; from a postcard by Walter Scott of Bradford *(Deborah Hannaford)*.

TRADESMEN AND WOMEN

THE BLACKSMITH, WHEELWRIGHT AND SAWYER

These crafts were closely allied, the blacksmith being required to produce all the ironwork for carts and wheels, and for the sledge or 'slide' which earlier had been Dartmoor's favoured method of transporting materials on farms.

The parish had at least five blacksmith's shops, the forges being at Widecombe, Venton, Ponsworthy and Poundsgate. This latter forge was sited at the present Post Office, previously a bakery.

Richard Kernick was the blacksmith at Widecombe when the present author was a boy and had been working there since the turn of the century. I remember well Percy Prouse and George Hambley, his partner. These two were more properly farriers, Fred Walters being a true blacksmith who actually created shoes and other ironwork in the forge.

I can recall working the bellows while Fred took and iron bar, and cut and hammered it to shape on the anvil, raised to a convenient height on a granite boulder. He then quenched the metal in a granite trough before the fire, before fitting the newly made shoe on to the horse's hoof. This was done while the shoe was still hot, imprinting itself on the horny part of the hoof amid much smoke.

It always amazed me that the horse didn't bolt at this point but Fred had a language all his own, talking to the horse with gutteral sounds which it seemed to understand as he hammered home the nails, filed them flat and trimmed the hoof.

The Southcombe Diaries relate that horses went either for new shoes or for 'removers', where the hoof had grown around the shoe, the horn trimmed and the shoe replaced.

Along with farriery, the blacksmith would also manufacture the general metalwork equipment found on the farms and the hearthside. Hinges and clasps of doors in our family cottage at Dunstone were made in Widecombe forge 150 years before. The smith also kept the roadmender's tools in trim, as the waywarden's accounts show: '1769. Paid John Stockman for new pick and sharping 3 end 4/4d.' Paid for Steeling a beal both ends 8d.'

Exhibiting some curious spelling the entries continue (1781): '2 poles for leavers 1/-; For pick hilfs 1/4d. For drawing of two ends of a pick 4d.; For 2 pegs and 2 church and ring nails 1/2d; For bend and nails for wheelbarrow 3/-; For steeling a sledge 1/2d. For mending a pick and sharping 6d.'

The wheelwright required an intimate knowledge of timber and the properties of each type. With infinite skill he would construct the component parts of the wheel: felloes, strakes, hub, etc. largely from oak and ash.

Most of this timber would be selected from tree trunks laid up for seasoning at the sawyer's yard. Orders would be placed for planks and spars of specific lengths and widths which the sawyer and his labourers would then produce.

It required a considerable degree of skill to manoeuvre a heavy trunk into position and then to cut planks of exact thicknesses from it. In the days before powered saws this was done using cross-cut saws with one man standing in a pit, another on the trunk above, drawing the massive saw up and down in turn.

Once the wheelwright had completed the wheel it would be taken to the forge for the fitting of the iron rim. A wheel with a five foot diameter would require a tyre 16 feet 6 inches long which would be made into a hoop slightly smaller than the circumference of the wheel.

The wheel itself would then be clamped to the binding stone, a huge circular slab of granite. The tyre would be heated in the forge and dropped over the rim of the wheel. Instantly it would be cooled by dousing it with water before the iron burned the wood, thus causing the tyre to contract, binding itself to the wheel.

It is difficult to comprehend the skill of these men who, by eye and hand alone, could create such perfect shapes from metal and wood.

The blacksmith also made brands for local farmers and the back door of the forge at Forder Bridge bears the imprint of many such brands. Colin Westwood, who supplied the photograph on page 92, wrote: 'The pony drift is held the first Friday in October. Each farmer separates foals, some for selling and some to go into an enclosure for branding. The irons were heated on a fire of 'blackwood' i.e. last year's brittle stems of gorse which had been swaled. Holly was never used for it was sticky and stuck to the iron.'

Peter Hannaford who was very skilled at branding used a mixture of copper sulphate and animal fat to spread on the new brand mark to help healing and to keep the flies off.

WIDECOMBE

Above left: Richard Kernick *(May Hambley)*; **centre:** Fred Walters and his wife. Fred was the last blacksmith of Widecombe *(Jack Prouse)*; **right:** Percy Prouse. *(Jack Prouse)*; **below:** Percy Prouse working at the forge *(Jack Prouse)*; **bottom left:** Widecombe forge 1939, Percy Prouse shoeing a horse *(Institute of Agricultural History)*; **bottom right:** Fred Walters shoeing Oliver Beard's horse *(Lily Hambley)*.

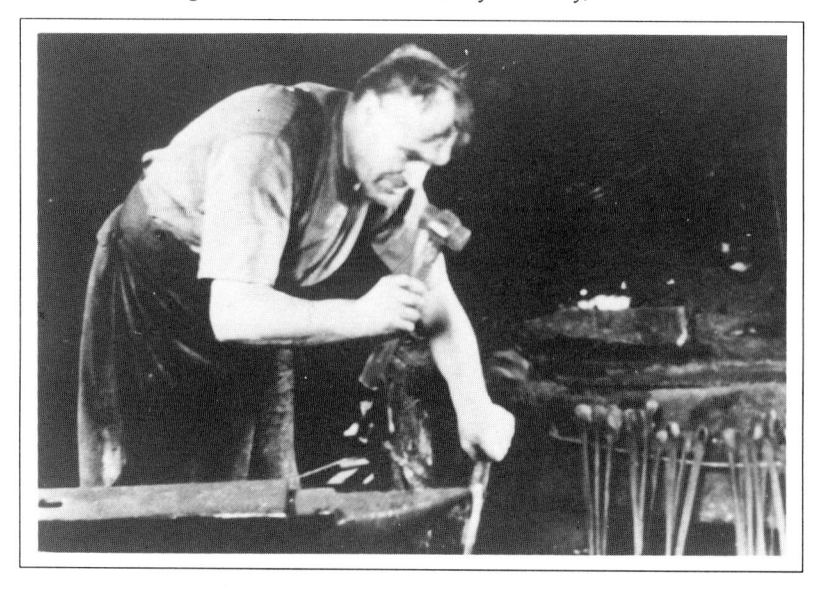

TRADESMEN AND WOMEN

A recent photograph of the forge at Ponsworthy.

Widecombe forge in the early 1920s, from a postcard by Chapman & Sons Note the thatched roof. *(Deborah Hannaford).*

Percy Prouse's sister, Annie, and George Hambley's sister, Alice, outside Widecombe forge in the 1940s. Note the edge of the wheelbinding stone on the right. *(May Hambley).*

WIDECOMBE

Above: Richard Kernick (in cap) and Fred Walters fitting an iron rim to a cartwheel, in the 1920s. The wheelbinding stone was later broken up during changes to the shop. *(Lily Hambley).*

Left: Brands on the door of the forge at Forder Bridge, Ponsworthy. Bessie French hazards a guess at identification: L = Leaman or Langdon; H = Hill or Hamlyn; JN = John Nosworthy or Norrish; C = Caunter or Cleave; S = Stephens; IC = H. Chaffe; M = Mann. Cattle were sometimes branded on the horn so the small 's' may have been used for that purpose. *(Colin Westwood).*

Below: Interior of Widecombe forge in recent times.

TRADESMEN AND WOMEN

The wedding of George Hambley to Lily Kernick. 19 June 1924. *(May Hambley).* 1. Jessie Hambley; 2 unknown; 3. unknown; 4. unknown; 5. Alice Warren; 6. Percy Prouse; 7. Mary Hext; 8. Louise Palmer; 9. Lily Gough (née Warren); 10. Brian Prouse; 11. Ethel Prowse (née Kernick); 12. Rosa Prowse (née Kernick); 13. Emily Kernick; 14. unknown; 15. unknown; 16. Cecil Churchward; 17. George Hambley; 18. Lily Hambley (née Kernick); 19. Stephen Hambley; 20. Mary Hambley; 21. Cyril Warren; 22. Ena Prowse; 23. Joan Prowse; 24. John Prouse; 25. Dorothy Prowse; 26. Wilfred Hext; 27. Eliza Kernick; 28. Richard Kernick.

PERCY CHARLES AND ROSA FLORENCE PROUSE

In response to the author's enquiry concerning the last blacksmith who worked in the parish, Jack Prouse, his son, wrote the following letter:

'Percy Prouse was born on 15 November 1891 at Ponsworthy being the youngest of ten children of John Lock Prouse and Frances Mary Prouse (née Nosworthy).

He attended school at Leusdon where Joshua Bancroft, a strict disciplinarian, was the master. His mother arranged for him to have piano lessons and I often heard him relate how she at times had to stand behind him with a cane to ensure that he did his practice. He used to say that, although at the time he did not appreciate it, he was always grateful to her as his subsequent knowledge and love of music made a big difference to him in later life. Upon leaving school he started work in the gardens at Spitchwick House. His brother-in-law, Harry Cleave, was then the head gardener.

Dad was appointed organist of Widecombe-in-the-Moor Parish Church in 1909, he was then about 18 years old, and he remained in that position, with the exception of his time in military service during the First World War, until shortly before his death on 25th June 1956 - some 47 years. As a young man his musical ability was in great demand and he used to play solo piano for numerous dances at Widecombe, Leusdon and other local villages.

During the First World War he joined the 5th Battalion of the Devonshire Regiment serving in India, Palestine and France. His army trade was a Farrier which I think he must have learnt after he enlisted. His work entailed shoeing far more mules than horses. He often related just how troublesome some of the mules had been.

On 30th March 1916 he married my mother Rosa Florence Kernick, the fourth of five daughters of Richard and Eliza Kernick of Widecombe-in-the-Moor. He was married in uniform whilst on a very short leave and sailed for India shortly afterwards. Mr Richard Kernick owned and worked the Blacksmith and Ironmongery business. One of Dad's older brothers, Frank, had some years previously married one of Mum's older sisters, Ethel. Frank died in 1917.

Whilst abroad Dad played the bass drum in the 5th Devon's band. A large photograph of that band is preserved at the Devon Regiment Museum, Topsham Barracks, Exeter. He was also in demand at the piano at various Officers' and NCO's mess functions. The battalion came back to France where they had a rough time. Dad developed pneumonia and was returned to the UK. He was in hospital in Scotland when the Armistice was signed. Upon demobilisation he returned to Widecombe to work for his father-in-law, Mr Kernick, as farrier and assisting the blacksmith in making and repairing agricultural implements and with general blacksmithing work.

They made all the horseshoes for their own use and even sold some to other farriers. I, their only child, was born on 16th July 1920. Dad's father, John Lock Prouse, was killed at Higher Dunstone Farm, Widecombe-in-the-Moor on 23rd November the same year whilst on his way to his home at Ponsworthy from his work at Natsworthy. The horse, drawing the trap in which my grandfather was travelling, bolted during a bad thunderstorm. The trap overturned, he was thrown out and killed.

By the mid to late 1920s Mr Kernick owned two cars. The one licensed as a 'Hackney Carriage' was driven by my father and used as a hire car. The other was licensed 'Private' and used in connection with the business. That was driven by George Hambley another son-in-law who had married Mr Kernick's youngest daughter Lily. Wednesday was Market Day at Newton Abbot. Dad, as with others, had his regular customers, five or six farmers' wives complete with the baskets of eggs, butter, cream, poultry and other farm produce.

During the middle to late 1930s my mother became very involved in the social life of the village, organising concerts, whist drives, etc. She, with her sisters Lily and Emily, had also built up the summer tourist side of Mr Kernick's business selling pottery, souvenirs, postcards, brasses etc. which entailed very long hours at the shop for all of them during the summer months. Dad's recreation was to talk to his friends or have the odd game of cards at one of the two local inns.

Mr Kernick died on 13th January 1940 and Mrs Kernick died on 22nd, nine days later. The business was then split. The summer tourist side was left to my mother and her two sisters, whilst the blacksmith and ironmongery side was left to the two sons-in-law, namely George Hambley and my father. Their business declined as farmers replaced their horses with tractors. Motor mechanics rather than blacksmiths were then in demand.

My mother died on 25th May 1951 aged 57 years. Her passing dealt Dad a very severe blow. However he continued on. His niece, Ena, looked after him for the next five years until he died on 25th June 1956. He was 64. Mum and Dad are both interred in the churchyard at Widecombe-in-the-Moor. Their grave is by the north east corner of the church near the vestry window.'

TRADESMEN AND WOMEN

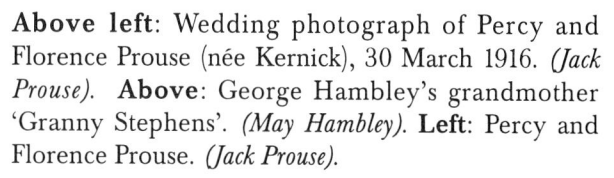

Above left: Wedding photograph of Percy and Florence Prouse (née Kernick), 30 March 1916. *(Jack Prouse)*. **Above**: George Hambley's grandmother 'Granny Stephens'. *(May Hambley)*. **Left**: Percy and Florence Prouse. *(Jack Prouse)*.

Above: Eliza Kernick serving in the shop. *(May Hambley)*.

Left: The Kernick sisters, late 1930s, l-r: Lily (Mrs Hambley); Mary; Emily; Ethel (Mrs Frank Prowse); Rosa (Mrs Percy Prowse). *(Jack Prouse)*.

WIDECOMBE

Mrs and Mrs Kernick and three daughters outside their new shop and petrol station, from a postcard by Chapman & Son, postmarked 1935. *(Deborah Hannaford)*.

Kernick's shop c. 1930s; note the grass sale posters. *(May Hambley)*.

Below left: Kernick's pottery store, reached by the steps down between the petrol pumps. This was once the implement store for the forge. From a photograph by J.M. Fisher & Co. *(May Hambley)*.

Below: A bill of sale, 1935.

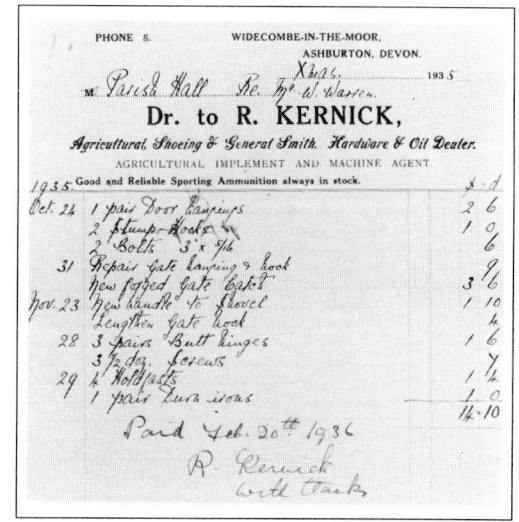

TRADESMEN AND WOMEN

THE MILLER

The Mesolithic people (8000–4000 BC) were hunter-gatherers, surviving by what they could forage from the land, pounding seeds of primitive types of cereal grasses into 'flour'. Tom Greeves has suggested the small cup-like depressions on the surface of the Dun Stone could have been produced in this way.

Later stone bowls were used for this purpose. Such a mortar, found at Corndon, is in the possession of Tony Beard. This small octagonal mortar, seven inches in diameter, is possibly of domestic use. A more sophisticated method of grinding corn was the quern, used from ancient times in the Middle East. The simplest form of quern involved two stones, one grinding upon the surface of the other and being rotated by a simple wooden handle. An upper stone of such a device was found in the Webburn (see photograph on page 100) and was cut with a series of grooves running outward from its centre, similar to millstones found in powered mills. As these hand mills had a limited life-span, and remained largely unchanged in design for centuries, it is almost impossible to accurately date them.

At Hutholes (see page 26) there is another relic associated with the production of flour. Here was discovered a small building specifically constructed to dry the grains of corn before milling. Such was the climate on Dartmoor that grains could not be dried satisfactorily in the fields. The building has a raised platform into which penetrate two flues from fireplaces or kilns set at their entrances. Warm air and smoke would enter the flues and rise up through the stored grain, thus drying it. At a later date one of the kilns was altered in order to assist in the malting process.

The medieval watermill used the power of a fast-flowing stream to turn the millstones connected through a series of wooden cogs. In Widecombe, as elsewhere, such mills belonged to the lord of the manor and under law the community had to take their corn to the manor mill for grinding, for which they paid a fee to the lord.

There are numerous references in historic documents to a 'messuage' between the west side of Widecombe churchyard and the 'way' (road), and in 1687 an indenture states 'All corn and grain to be ground at the manorial mill.' And again in 1713 'they are to grind all the corn grain or mault spent or used on the premises of the mills of the sd. S. Wotton called the Norrale Mills parcel of the manor of Widecombe.'

From medieval times such mills were commonplace and several sites can be identified within the parish. There are possibly two in Widecombe, and others at Cockingford, Ponsworthy and Jordan, all within a mile radius. There was also a mill at Babeny, the outline of its ruin can be seen on the right bank of the Wallabrook, just above the bridge. An ancient lower millstone is set into the ground directly in front of a barn door. Of this mill William Crossing wrote: 'In 1302 or 1303 the holders of the tenements in the Forest built a mill at Babeny at their own cost, the king supplying the timber, which was felled in his wood. At this mill each tenant had to do service, as appears from an account of the prince's manors of the 2nd March 1344.'

The last grist mill to operate on Dartmoor was at Cockingford and the author saw this mill in operation, watching the water race down a long wooden launder and on to the turning wheel. The whirling stones turned and hot meal fell from the shute into a waiting sack.

The mill was destroyed on the morning of 4 August 1938. A great storm broke over the moor and the waters of the East Webburn surged downstream carrying all before. Debris piled up at the single span bridge at Cockingford, flooding the mill and damaging the millwheel and launder beyond repair.

The late Elizabeth Gawne pointed out to the present author that the mill machinery was still in place at Ponsworthy Mill, and the photographs on page 100, taken with the permission of the late Sam Cannon, show its remains. This mill dates back to at least 1281 when it was recorded as Pauntesford. In 1544 it is recorded that the mill was sold by John, Earl of Bath, to Richard Langworthy of Withecombe.

At some time before it ceased operation earlier this century the mill had gears and belts added to its power-train in order to drive a power saw and thresher.

Upriver from Ponsworthy is Jordan Mill, now an attractive residence. The Jordan or Dewdon Mills were sold in 1602 and described as 'One Greiste Mille and a Fulling Mille.' The fulling process was an essential part of wollen cloth production requiring a plentiful supply of water.

WIDECOMBE

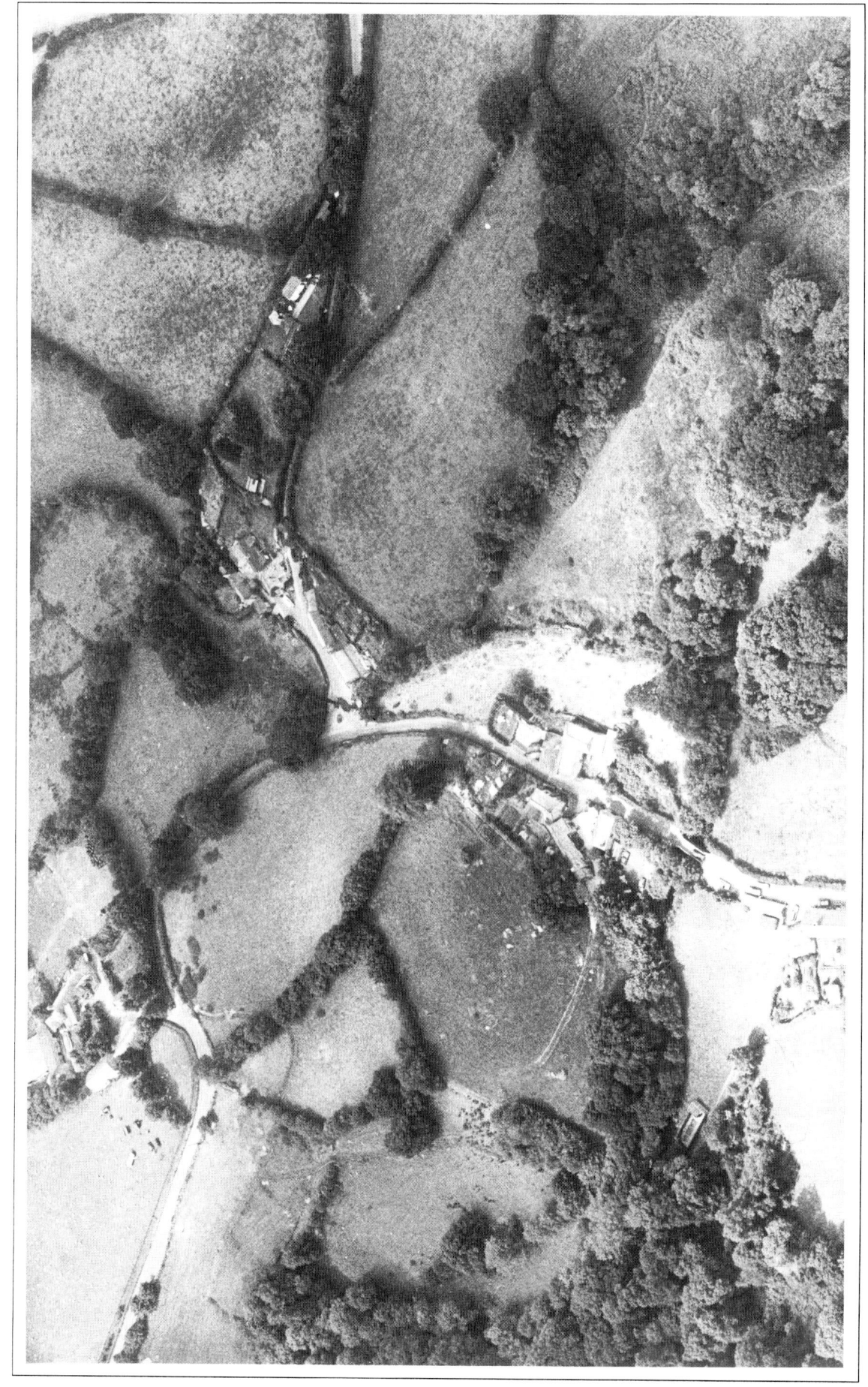

Aerial view of Ponsworthy village. The shoemaker's house and the mill are sited in the cluster of buildings in the centre of the photograph to the right of the lane, with rose cottage, the bakehouse and the wheelwright's shop on the left.

TRADESMEN AND WOMEN

Ponsworthy mill from a drawing dated 22 November 1856 by Frederick Foot (1831-1908). *(Torquay Natural History Society)*.

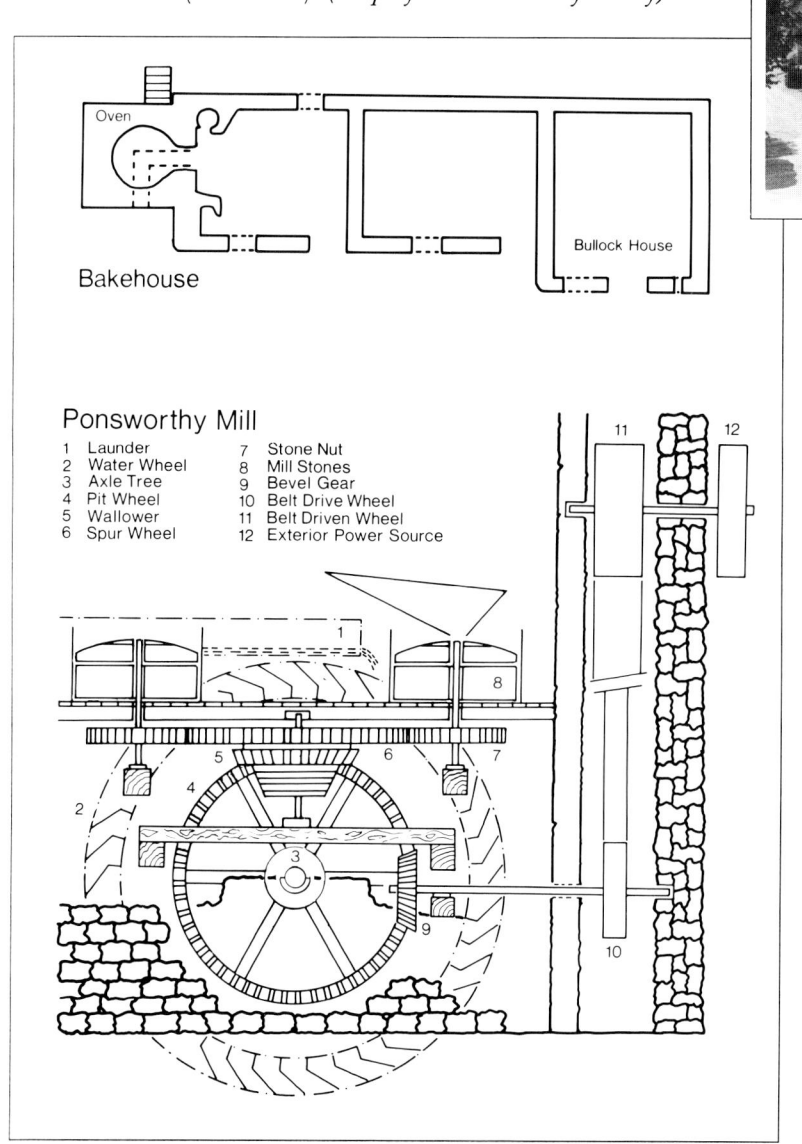

Ponsworthy Mill House today.

Ponsworthy Mill
1 Launder
2 Water Wheel
3 Axle Tree
4 Pit Wheel
5 Wallower
6 Spur Wheel
7 Stone Nut
8 Mill Stones
9 Bevel Gear
10 Belt Drive Wheel
11 Belt Driven Wheel
12 Exterior Power Source

Plan of the Bakehouse at Ponsworthy and the mill wheel and grinding apparatus at Ponsworthy Mill.

99

WIDECOMBE

Above left: upper-stone of a quern (top view) found in the river Webburn at Ponsworthy. **Left**: Sam Cannon and two upper-stones from Ponsworthy Mill. **Right**: The remains of Cockingford waterwheel, destroyed by a storm in 1938. Note the long launder running up towards the rear of the wheel.

The interior of Ponsworthy Mill showing the spurwheel with the wallower below, turned by the pitwheel attached by an axle to the waterwheel.

TRADESMEN AND WOMEN

This photograph by Robert Burnard, grandfather of Lady Sylvia Sayer, shows the miller's cart at Widecombe in 1890. The small girl on the cart is Burnard's daughter Dorothy who married Revd K.A. Lake, one time curate to the Revd Sabine Baring-Gould. *(Lady Sylvia Sayer)*.

Jordan Mill House.

WIDECOMBE

THE BAKER

There were a number of bakeries in the parish, the earliest possibly at Ponsworthy, connected with the mill there. Leases for the bakehouse survive dating from 1654, 1687 and 1745 but John Tollick is the only known person described as 'baker and miller,' in 1855-57. Afterwards he moved to Lower Dunstone Farm which became known as Tollicks from that time.

The bakery stands back from the road partly behind the wheelhouse, recently renovated as a private dwelling. The original bakehouse was 15 feet long and 12 feet wide, built with the oven constructed at one end. Later an additional section was added, of identical size, known as the bullock house, indicating that the bakery had by then ceased operation.

The oven is constructed in a similar fashion to those traditionally found in longhouses and church houses but on a larger scale and with additional features. It comprises a large hearth and chimney with a domestic bread oven built into the right hand side. At the back of the hearth is the entrance to the 'commercial' oven, a short passage opening out into a circular baking area with a diameter of approximately 5 feet, sides a foot high, with a domed roof. The oven is set at waist height for ease of operation. An iron plate closed the entrance. A cavity beneath the oven leads to the prover and provides an exit for ashes. Above the oven was a store room, accessed by exterior steps at the back of the building.

Ovens of the size described were known as sack ovens, a sack being 200 pounds of flour, to which was mixed 3 pounds of yeast, 3.5 pounds of salt, and 5 bucketsful of water. This provided sufficient dough to fill the oven for one baking.

Eddy Hunt, baker of Buckfastleigh, who used this type of oven commercially, described its use: The oven was prepared the night before, with three faggots (bound bundles of sticks), one on each side and one across the top. When these had burned down the ashes were raked towards the entrance and another faggot added. In total six or seven faggots would be burned to attain the right temperature.

The first ashes out would be raked into the prover and used to raise the dough.

Buns and rolls went into the oven first, taking about twenty minutes to cook, these with smaller loaves in tins went round the outside. After it had been washed clean with a mop, larger loaves were placed directly on to the floor in the centre of the oven, taking about an hour to cook.

Other bakeries in the parish were at Linchaford, Poundsgate and Widecombe (behind Southcombe Villas). Andrew Harvey was the baker at Widecombe in the 1920s, supplying local needs and delivering throughout the area twice weekly. Later he and his sister, May, moved to Wayside where he ran the cafe and May the Post Office.

The bakery at Poundsgate (in what was to become the Post Office) is now a private residence but still retains the original oven. This operated between the 1860s and 1930s but that date at which it first came into use is unknown.

The bakehouse at Ponsworthy.

TRADESMEN AND WOMEN

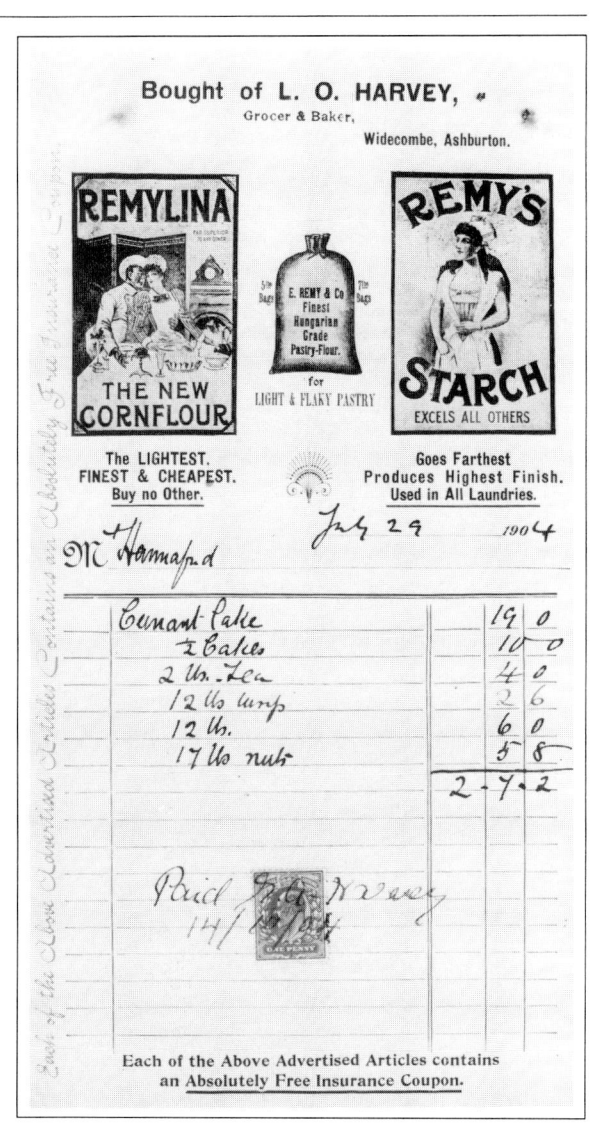

Top left: the bread oven set in the side of the fireplace in the Ponsworthy bakehouse. **Lower left**: the prover, set below the sack oven, where the dough was set to rise. **Above right**: a bill of sale from Harvey's bakery *(Hermon French)*. **Below**: Andrew Harvey and Sidney Bray (in cap, later a postman), with the bread delivery van that took over from horses. *(Joan Hambleton)*.

THE CORDWAINER

At a parish meeting in 1854 it is recorded 'a boy incapable of Farm labour named Elias Norrish aged about Fifteen years requiring to be apprenticed to be taught a trade.' Charles Warren of Ponsworthy being present agreed to take and instruct the boy in the trade of a cordwainer.

'Elias Norrish is hereby bound to Charles Warren of Ponsworthy to be taught the Trade of Boot and Shoe Maker to be clothed and fed and supported by him the said Charles Warren until he has attained the age of 21 years - the parish engaging to pay £7 to the said Charles Warren at the time of his taking him in, £7 when the said Elias Norrish shall have served half his time, and remaining £4 when he shall have attained the age of 21 years and have completed his apprenticeship.'

The making of boots and shoes was an ancient trade vital to the community and it died out, along with so many other rural crafts, only when machine made shoes became commonplace during the nineteenth century. William Crossing wrote: 'The Village Cordwainer too is disappearing before the march of 'ready made' boots, or when he exists, is more often only a 'mender of soles'.

The moormen's boots would be made to last a lifetime, with the blacksmith putting the finishing touches (called 'tackling') to new boots, fitting them with iron plates or hobnails. A woman would wear pattens, a form of sandal with a wooden sole which would lift her feet and long pinafore clear of the mud and wet.

The Warrens ran a very successful boot and shoe business at Ponsworthy for many decades; among their customers were the Hannafords, as related in the Southcombe Diaries. H.H. Hannaford, writing in February 1902, made sure that 'a Nosworthy Junior' was fitted out with the proper footwear, 'scoots and toe plates and nails 6d.' when he started employment at Southcombe.

The Dartmoor tradition of step-dancing, its own variation of clog dancing, made use of the heavy footwear worn by the working people. Crossing says of Edward Caunter, a celebrated practitioner of this form of dancing:

'He would spring into the middle of the kitchen, and favour those present with a specimen of his ability as a step dancer, and prove himself a nimble performer, too, not withstanding that he carried seven pounds weight of leather and iron on his feet.'

Step dancing was a regular pastime in kitchens and the tap rooms of inns 'and zometimes a man 'ud 'ave a scoot loose in e's boot, an' the'd be a brave rattlin, sure nuff.'

The shoemaker's house, Ponsworthy c. 1900. *(Jack Prouse)*.

TRADESMEN AND WOMEN

THE POST OFFICE AND LETTER CARRIER

The delivery of letters is centuries old but the modern Post Office and the introduction of the Royal Mail was the brainchild of Rowland Hill. With the advent of the Penny Black stamp in 1840 the first regularised mail service came into being.

Even so the rural service was slow to develop and it was not until Anthony Trollope, the novelist and post official (1815-1822), was appointed the Commissioner for Devon that things improved. It is said that he visited most houses in the county and in the course of two years established a network of letter carriers.

Post Office records give 1855 as the first reference to Widecombe which then came under Newton Abbot, 12 miles distant. The nearest money order office was at Ashburton.

The first Post Office, also a bakery, was housed in the building known as Southcombe Villas, beside the road from Dunstone. Interestingly *White's Gazetteer* for 1850 states 'Post Office at Diana Lemon's' -her correct name, Dinah Leaman, appearing in the 1851 census along with her occupation 'Letter Receiver.'

The present Post Office and village store is over a hundred yards away and between times it was housed at the Wayside Cafe on the far side of the green.

To facilitate the collection of mail, wall boxes were introduced in 1857-58, the idea originating with the Postmaster of Plymouth. A wall box at Venton is of the type erected between 1881 and 1904. There were three variations, large, medium and small, and each included the innovation of an enamelled indicator showing the hours of collection. The Venton box is the medium size and is believed to date from around 1895. The small type is built into the wall at Dunnabridge Pound Farm. The author remembers an Edward VII box at Dunstone but it was updated many years ago.

In the early years of the present century the postman would walk out from Ashburton with the Widecombe mail, wait while it was delivered and take back any outgoing mail in the evening. Tony Beard recalls a later arrangement: 'The post was brought out from Ashburton by pony and trap and in about 1924 they used a Renault van, father remembers that the mail van driver was Jack Johnson and he would stay all day and then take the post back with him in the afternoon. He would spend quite a part of the day at the Rugglestone and was a bit 'worse for wear; when it came time to go home, and he would often say to father "Yer, Sid, you kin drive 'n as far as Paunsry (Ponsworthy)." So father used to drive it and he was only about 13 years old at the time!'

From Widecombe Post Office there were at least three rounds but not all farms had a delivery to their door in the early days. The Dymond Diaries make the point that they either had to meet the postman or go to Widecombe to collect their letters. It can be assumed that Tunhill, Scobitor and other outlying farms had to operate a similar system, either listening out for the postman's whistle as he walked his round, or collecting the mail from Widecombe.

The diaries record for 29 June 1871 that: 'The Mother, Carrie, Effie and Mabel went for a walk. They went to Dunston to give 12 letters to the Postman whose whistle we heard before we reached the road so we had to run after him. When Carrie who had to do the running caught up with him he kindly enquired "Have you been bawlin' after me Miss Dymond?" Miss Dymond had certainly called "Postman" once, but she could not exactly say yes to his question.'

Widecombe can boast of an interesting role in postal history which is both a monument to the rural postman and a condemnation of the Post Office authorities. James Beard was born in 1861 and became an auxilliary postman in 1872 when he was eleven years old. It was the usual practice for the Post Office to employ boys no younger than fourteen years.

Young Master Beard was taken before a magistrate in Ashburton and made to swear an oath to handle the mail with complete honesty and security. The magistrate was perturbed by these proceedings and declared he would never administer the oath to such a young person again.

The boy was fitted out with a uniform, cap, overcoat, a mackintosh cape and, of course, a bag for carrying the mail. Parcels were carried as well as letters but there was a limit on size and weight. A wallet containing stamps was also carried, three shilling's worth of stamps which would be checked from time to time to ensure that the value of stamps or coins always balanced. Any shortfall was made up by the postman.

As an auxilliary the round, done on foot, was supposed to take all morning - in bad weather it might easily take a great deal longer.

In 1931 James Beard retired at the age of seventy and did not receive any pension from the Post Office despite his 59 years of service. He died in 1942 aged eighty-one and was laid to rest in Widecombe churchyard.

Walter Butlin, postman, outside the Tavistock Inn c.1890. *(Marjorie and Geoff Weymouth).*

These facts were passed on to Iris Woods by Bessie Beard, daughter of James.

It is not known who followed Dinah Leaman at the Post Office but by the turn of the century Owen Harvey was postman, delivering the mail on horseback. His wife was postmistress, running the Post Office and village shop, while their son Andrew ran the bakery sited behind the shop, and their daughter May was assistant to Mrs Bates at the Church House school.

After the death of their parents May and Andrew moved to Wayside where May became postmistress.

It was quite a family business for May Harvey's niece, Joan Hambleton, relates: 'The outlying farms and houses had their mail delivered by my grandfather and mother, Louise Harvey, on horseback, sometimes in the winter when the weather was so severe the horses would not face into a snowstorm and I have heard Mum say she would have to back the horse so it would not be facing into the snow, but the mail always got delivered.'

Joan recalls that the author Beatrice Chase was so convinced that the local Post Office read her mail she had it delivered in a special sealed bag from Ashburton. When the regular postman was on leave, in this instance Sidney Bray, Joan would stand in.

Along with the mail the Post Office also operated a small savings bank. Joan recalls 'A young lady would save a small sum each week and pay the money into her acount. Eventually she left the village to obtain employment in another part of the country, but one day her mother arrived with her daughter's saving book and asked to withdraw three pounds. When she was told that only her daughter could make the withdrawal and that from the Post Office where she now lived, the mother became very angry and said that the money was not at any other office, it had definitely been paid into Widecombe, she had seen it put in the drawer...'

In May Harvey's time Widecombe did not have an automatic telephone exchange and May was responsible for seeing it was manned seven days a week, 24 hours a day. Sidney Beard recalled 'In the 1920s there was only one line from Widecombe and one from Poundsgate and anyone wanting a vet or doctor would ride to the P.O. and a call would be put through for them to Ashburton or Moretonhampstead.

A wealthy industrialist bought Blackaton Manor and asked the Post Office to instal a telephone line all the way from Ponsworthy. They refused to do so at their own cost and so the industrialist had his agent send a succession of telegrams addressed to him at Widecombe. It was a statutory obligation of the Post Office to deliver telegrams immediately and each one required Mrs Harvey to hire a taxi in order to deliver them to Blackaton right away. The Post Office installed the line. Several other dwellings now use the same installation

TRADESMEN AND WOMEN

The original Widecombe Post Office, Southcombe Villas. James Beard, auxilliary postman 1872-1931 reporting for duty - from a postcard by Owen Harvey. *(Elisabeth Stanbrook).*

Southcombe Villas today, originally the village Post Office and bakery.

The Victorian letterbox at Dunnabridge Pound Farm.

An old postcard of Manor Cottages, the well, and the present Post Office.

WIDECOMBE

Smithhill, c. 1920; later renamed Wayside it became the Post Office and the Wayside Cafe. *(Iris Woods)*.

The old village sign in the 1930s with the Wayside Cafe and Post Office - from a postcard by F. Frith & Co. *(Iris Woods)*.

Aerial view of Poundsgate's original Post Office and Bakery with Lake Farm behind.

TRADESMEN AND WOMEN

Left: Mr Jones, postman, outside the Wayside Post Office c. 1940. *(May Hambley)*.

Below left: Mr Muggeridge, postman. He walked with the mail to and from Ashburton, staying all day in the hut behind Southcombe Villas. *(Joan Hambleton)*.

Below: May Harvey, schoolmistress and postmistress. *(Joan Hambleton)*.

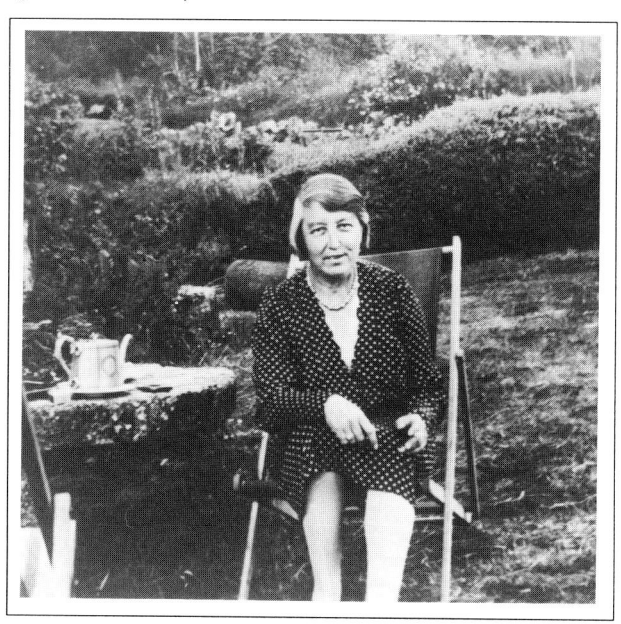

Above left: Poundsgate Post Office and bakery. Mrs Webber stands next to the two postmen, Mr Hannaford on foot and George Widecombe astride the pony. *(Marjorie and Geoff Weymouth)*.

Above: May Harvey, postmistress and her new Austin c. 1930. *(Joan Hambleton)*.

Left: Collecting the mail at Wayside in the 1930s. The woman standing in the centre of the group is Mrs Follett, May Harvey to her right. *(Joan Hambelton)*.

WIDECOMBE

THE TINNER

The history of the tin industry on Dartmoor is a story of epic proportions which has left its mark over the whole of the moor. The industry is covered in more detail in the author's *Dartmoor Stone*, and in works by Tom Greeves, acknowledged as the expert in this field.

The tinner was literally a law unto himself, having protection under the ancient Stannary Law, to which Sovereign rights were secondary. Miners attended their own courts at the four Devon Stannary Towns: Chagford, Ashburton, Plympton and Tavistock. Dynham's survey in 1566 of Natsworthy Manor states 'There be mynes of tynne within this manor but the lordes have no toll thereof because ye customes of Stanary of Devon is to the contrary.'

The eminence of miners is reflected in the Burial Registers of Widecombe where tinners only have their trade stated after their name:

'1617 Apter, Gabriell, was buried at Ilsington, who was spoyled in a tin work 24 Oct; 1618 Smerdon, George, kild in a tin worke 14 Apr; 1706 Humphrey, William a tinner 27 June; 1711 Wills, Edward, tinner 4 Nov; 1799, Roberts, John aged 64 years 21 Apr.' (written in pencil after this entry 'A Miner').

The site of several tin works can be identified from historical documents, such as the lease between 'John Bourgchier, kt, Lord of Fitzwarren and two tinners Christopher Prous and Richard Hamlyn' dated 1 January 1514. The bounds of the work were 'an acre of land lying in the waste next to Dertemeta in the manor of Spechewyke, between the spring there called Hangerwille on the south and the water of Derta on the west and Smethaford on the north and the way leading from Smethaford as far as Greneway on the east. Also a myll there called a blowyng myll and knakking myll with the weir and the stream of water flowing to the said myll which Christopher and Richard lately built there.' This land today comprises Badgers Holt and the adjacent car park.

Dynham's survey refers also to 'the aforesaid lands in th' occupacion or tenure of Peter Langworthy lyeth in the north parte of the Churchway that lyeth between Blackadon vyllage and th' inheritance land of the said Peter in the Sowth-est parte, and the walls of an old house sumtyme a blowing house lyenge without the hedges of the said ground.'

Hermon French surveyed this site of which little remained but an outline. He also looked at a blowing house on Blackaton Ball Moor below Grendon Bridge.

Hermon had a document dated 1759 setting out the tin bounds covering the west flank of Hameldown in the manor of Jordan, the 'Head Weare' (reservoir) being under Stoneslade Tor. Here, just over the ridge, can be seen one of the finest examples of a tin streaming operation on Dartmoor. The crescent-shaped reservoir still fills with water in winter just as it did centuries ago when the tinners would release the water down the 'gert' to wash away soil and expose the tin beneath.

Many relics of the tin trade can be found throughout the parish. A float from the bottom of a blowing house furnace lies beside the road at Chittleford where the excavations are still known as the Chittleford Works. A field close by is called Mill Meadow.

Within the Ancient Tenements mould stones can be seen at Postbridge and in the wall at Riddon, where tinners diverted the river in search of tin. A large boulder in Soussons wall was used three times as a base for the stamps. Tom Greeves had it from John Hamlyn that there was a 'blower' below Runnage Bridge.

Other works existed at Brimpts, opposite Dartmeet. The word 'beam' or 'beme' is often associated with tin working and thus the Easterbremstebeme of old documents could describe the east tin works on Brimpts.

Further along the Dart at Week Ford are twin blowing houses with many mortar and mould stones among the ruins. Past Hexworthy into the valley of the Swincombe there are the ruins of another blowing house, also with a range of mortar and mould stones, and the only example of a crazing mill left on Dartmoor. This site is known as Gobbet, and previously may have been the site of Sweincombfoote tin works.

The parish of Widecombe was divided between the Stannary Courts of Chagford and Ashburton. It was to these two towns that tinners took their smelted ingots for assay, to be stamped and taxed.

TRADESMEN AND WOMEN

An aerial view of Hameldown showing the scars on the landscape left by tinners in previous centuries. The long cutting running up to the track (top left) to Hameldown Beacon is the result of openwork mining where the tinners followed the lode of tin up the hillside. Remains of the reservoir can also be seen top right of centre.

Left: tinners' reservoir on Hameldown.

Below left: granite float that once lay at the mouth of a tinner's furnace now lies beside the road at Chittleford.

Below: a triple mortar stone now lies outside the Wayside Cafe.

111

Sam Cannon farm labourer *(Barbara Norrish)*.

THE FARMER AND HIS LABOURER

Much of the information provided in this chapter is based on the writings contained in the Southcombe Diaries. These cover the last years of horse power, before mechanisation simplified cultivation and land clearance. Indeed the final entries in the last diary dated 1931 contain the note: 'November 17th. Jumbo [the workhorse] left last night and has not been heard of yet.'

Jumbo was one of several horses at Southcombe, others included Prince, Boxer and Shamrock. The lost skills involved in working with horses are a lamentable fact of their passing. Jumbo, by the way, was found four days later 'on the commons'.

The economy of the moorland farms was interwoven with the rights that were attached to each landholding, not to the occupiers. Such rights allowed the farmer to keep stock on the commons and included the right to take turf, ferns and gorse, to quarry stone and to gather wood.

Ferns (bracken is referred to only as ferns) were used for bedding. The author can recall Mr Opie, who worked for William Warren at Lower Dunstone Farm, driving the cows up on to Dunstone Down in the mornings where he would scythe down an area of bracken, bringing it home in the evening in a net carried on his shoulders as he drove the cows back for milking.

The manor was very precise about this activity, recording in the 1872 court: 'We present that by custom of this Manor no fern should be cut before September in the Commons on the east side of the valley not before the 10th September on the west side.'

Geoff Weymouth told the author 'We used to cut ferns for bedding fetched from steep ground using a slide fitted with lades front and rear. The average countryman of my youth had the following approach to flora and fauna that was around them "If you can't eat it or sell it, ignore it or git rid ought."'

The right to cut peat and turf, turbary, was an essential for it provided fuel for the massive hearths which provided heating and on which (prior to the installation of ranges) all the cooking was done.

The cut slice of peat was known as a fag or vag and, again the Manor of Dunstone was precise in its instructions: '5th October 1897. At a Manor Court of this Manor held yesterday it was decided by the Commoners that every person permitted to cut fag or turf on the Manor Commons be required to mark in prominent letters his or her name or initials upon the spot whence the turf or fag is taken.'

There are many references to turf throughout the diaries and in 1931 they include: 'July 7th Sam (Cannon) Jack (Brown) and H (Hermon French) cutting turf on Ridge. Cut about 2000 fags. October 10th. Sam absent, Jack thatching last rick at Dockwell & help H to put away 1000 fags brought from Ridge by Miners lorry.'

Bill and Sam Miners were in the haulage business and were also engaged on the farm. Their names appear periodically in the diaries, helping out with shearing, thrashing, etc. and frequently taking out a horse and cart. They built up a thriving haulage business and Bill Miners may well have owned the first tractor in the parish, offering it for hire.

The most important right was that of pasturage and the amount of stock each farm could keep on the commons was governed by the number 'as they maye winter upon there holdyngs.' This limitation ensured good husbandry, for each farmer knew that he had to take animals off the commons in winter and feed and house them on the farm.

While stock grazed on the commons, the fields were used in the summer months to grow food to sustain the flocks and herds in winter. Many farms also held land off the moor, or bought grass keep on which to pasture stock before it was put on to the commons.

The agricultural economy was based on mixed farming, that is a flock of sheep, a score or so of cattle, and a few pigs and chickens. Southcombe was larger than the average Dartmoor farm as the returns for 1902 indicate: 'Cows 6, Bullocks 16, Yearlings 11, Calves 6 - Total 39; Ewes 73, Ewe Hogs 58 (1 dead), Weathers and Barreners 40, Lambs 92 - Total 263; Number of sheep shorn 261; Horses 4; Ponies 3.'

Stock and produce for sale were taken to Newton Abbot market. The sales accounts for Wednesday 22 January, 1902 show:

4lbs butter @ 1/4	5/4
2 doz. eggs @ 1/3	2/4
16 rabbits @ 7d	9/4
12 bags potatoes @ 4/-	£2.8.4d
Total	£3.5.0d

The owner, occupier or tenant of a moorland farm was a working farmer, labouring with his family and assisted by a minimum number of labourers, often apprentices. The workforce would be increased by hired hands at particular times of year, sheep-shearing and harvest.

WIDECOMBE

Geoff Weymouth recalled that there was a strong social hierarchy. The squire was addressed as Sir, his wife as Ma'am; the farmer as Mister or 'Maister' and his wife as Missus; to use the farmer's Christian name would result in instant dismissal. The labourers were known by their Christian names.

Herbert Henry Hannaford recorded his workers' names in the style: 'S. Hambley'. HHH's son, John, would write 'Stephen', leaving out the surname.

Stephen Hambley worked on Southcombe and Dockwell which were run together for a great many years. He was joined by Fred (Gough) and Cecil (Churchward), the latter who became the driver and mechanic when the first car arrived on the farm in 1920.

Other diary entries record everyday events: '10th Oct. 1902. Hen in hall hatched 7 chickens; 12 Oct. Daisy had 9 kittens; 3 Nov. Fly had 6 puppies.' And in 1925: 'Cecil to Newton, Second visit to dentist (gas); 13th May 4th visit to dentist; 27th May. 5th visit to dentist.'

On 9 August, 1902 the diary breaks forth into poetry:
 Held sportations and dancations
 In commemoration
 Of the Celebration
 Of the Coronation
 Of the jubiliation
 Of the nation.

The labourer was paid every other week on average for his work, and the hours were long. Rarely did the weather prevent the day's work going ahead and there are few entries 'about barn' which indicates a day on which the weather forced the men to take shelter. The wages were notoriously low but generally the labourer would at least be supplied with a tied cottage and, in some cases, produce from the farm.

From the 1920s onward a general scale of farm wages was introduced in Devon. This was based on a week of 50 hours, with work on Saturday (in excess of 6 hours) and Sunday, to be charged as mutually agreed. A male labourer aged 21 years or over was paid 32/6 per week, a female worker at 5p per hour. At the other end of the scale a boy apprentice aged 14-15 was paid 11/- per week and a girl 2d. per hour. Overtime rates were also fixed, varying according to age.

The labourer could turn his hand to most jobs on the farm with ease. In the winter he would be about the plough, followed by the harrow. Even in the wettest winters such work went ahead. Geoff Weymouth recalls that in wet weather they used to wear hessian sacks known then as 'Granna Begs'.

Ploughing on steep slopes caused the soil to creep down to the foot of the field and this resulted in 'drawing soil', shovelling the earth into a butt and taking it to the top of the field to be spread. Such butts could be a three-wheeled cart, or a cart with two wheels and a slide in front, or one wheel in front and two slides behind. Granite boulders in the way would be ploughed around or broken up, the land then dug using a 'twobill', a kind of pickaxe with a point at one end, the other end being flattened into a chopping edge.

The diaries record that in January 1927 W. Norrish was employed for a few days 'about rocks' and during this time the 'jumper and bar' were 'shaped and resharped' by the smith.

The penning of stock meant a continuous round of 'fraithing, steeping and gapping', the upkeep of hedges. Fraithing was the interweaving of cut branches with growing vegetation to create a stock-proof hedge. Steeping was stock-proofing using growing timber, cut partly through to ensure its continued growth, and laying it on to the hedge. Gapping was the repair of stone and earth-built hedges.

For many centuries the only fertiliser available was the dung from animals and ashes from the hearth. The alkaline ashes helped to balance the acidic moorland soil and ash houses were used to store the ash from domestic hearths. Few remain within the parish - a possible example survives at Babeny although this may be a goose-house.

The first artificial fertiliser was lime. Limestone was brought on packhorses to be burnt in makeshift limekilns to produce quicklime. From the evidence of field names such as 'Kiln Close' and 'Kiln Field' it was only on the larger farms of Broadaford, Wooder and Lizwell that this practice was followed. At Southcombe, apart from ashes and dung, waysoil was collected (the accumulation of washed-out earth and decaying vegetation from the edges of lanes). In more recent times commercial fertilisers were used on all farms.

There are numerous references in the diaries to 'turning water' - an old and common practice of running water over the fields to raise the temperature of the soil in order to induce an early crop.

The late Jack Brown provided the author with a description of sowing by hand. This 'broadcast' method remained essentially unchanged since earliest times. The sower carried the seed in a pan or basket strapped around his waist. He took three steps and threw a handful of seed to the right, then three steps and a handful to the left, and so on across the field. Part of the secret of successful sowing was to walk at a steady unvarying pace, and for the sower to fix his eyes on an object at the far side of the field and to walk straight towards it.

Among the crops grown on Dartmoor farms were mangels, turnips, swedes, potatoes, cabbages, broccoli, cauliflower, kale, oats, wheat and barley. Grass was also a crop, being sown and harvested as hay for winter feed.

Apart from hay the 'letting of grass' was also an important annual event. Sometimes this was a result of the farmer 'easing up', reducing his work commitments; often it was a sign of bad times and it could be embarrassing to be seen to be selling one's grass keep. Such sales were usually held at auction.

In early times cereal crops and hay were cut by hand, men walking in teams staggered across the field, scything the crop and leaving it to be gathered into stooks. The photograph on page 119 shows that scythes were still in use well into the present century.

An interesting field name on Bunhill is 'Day Moth', a corruption of 'Day's Moweth', that is a field that could be cut by hand in a day.

Once cut, whether hay or corn, it would be gathered in and stacked in ricks which were then thatched against the weather. Rushes were often used for this purpose. Fred Gough who worked at Southcombe for many years eventually built up a thriving business as a thatcher.

A diary entry of 11 September 1919: 'HHH drove horses in reaper to Venton.' This may be the earliest reference to a horse-drawn mechanical reaper in the parish.

Extra men were taken on for the corn harvest and again when it came time to thrash (or thresh) the corn in the ricks. A diary entry for 30 December records: 'W. & S. Miners, H. Hannaford, W. & A. Hern, J. Horton, T. Bate, M. Mann, thrashing.'

In 1923 an engine was brought in to help with the thrashing, before that the thrasher was driven by horses. The only horse gear known to the author lay outside a barn a Great Dunstone. There is a roundhouse on Lizwell Farm where the horse gear would operate next to the thrashing floor - see the photograph on page 117.

An entry in the Dymond Diaries on 1 October, 1873 records the excitement at thrashing time: 'Allie and Effie were much interested in it, and finally took up their residence in the barn with books and eatables. The thrashing machine is moved by four horses in an apparently separate shed, and the noise there is not nearly so loud as in the barn. Tomorrow we are going to winnow. Today (2 October) nearly all the oats that were thrashed yesterday were winnowed in a winnowing machine borrowed from Scobetor, but though the noise is not so deafening as that of the thrashing machine it is not so interesting to watch.'

Geoff Weymouth writes that 'I do indeed remember horses driving barn machinery. As a young boy (early 1930s) I watched the operation many times. Four horses were shackled to four wooden arms and the horseman used to sit (mostly) on a stationary 3 foot square platform in the centre. The machinery consisted of a barr thresher, reed comber, chaff cutter, saw bench and oat crusher.'

The water mill at Ponsworthy also drove such machinery.

A flock of sheep has always been of prime importance to the Dartmoor farmer. Writing in the eighteenth century Vancouver says 'on the commons belonging to the parish of Widecombe... estimated by a gentleman residing in the neighbourhood, to be no less than 14,000 sheep.'

In those days there was a thriving woollen industry with numerous mills at Chagford, Ashburton and Buckfastleigh. Today only one mill remains in operation.

Sylvester Mann told the author that the sheep 'kept on the moor were known as Widecombes, now known as Whiteface Dartmoors.'

Sheep had to be dipped in order to rid them of parasites. Such dips existed at Southcombe, Lizwell and Corndon farms, and also at Stannon Newtake, Postbridge. All farms used one or other of these dips and sheep had to be dipped by 20 July, the local policeman watching to see that this was done.

Relics of the woollen industry can be seen in the sheepfold near Hartland Tor the sheepwash on Brimpts and the sheepstell under Laughter Tor.

Beatrice Chase wrote: 'every man on Dartmoor can farm, therefore nearly every man on Dartmoor can shear sheep. Every man who can shear sheep can cut his brother man's hair.' The author's grandfather frequently had his hair cut in this manner by Jack Brown of Lower Dunstone.

Cows were kept to provide milk for the production of butter. A small amount of milk was consumed, some sold to neighbours and some kept for the making of cream. The late Eric Hemery, author, is not the only one to remember the sumptuous cream teas provided by the Hannafords of Headland, thick cream piled high on splits topped with delicious whortleberry jam.

WIDECOMBE

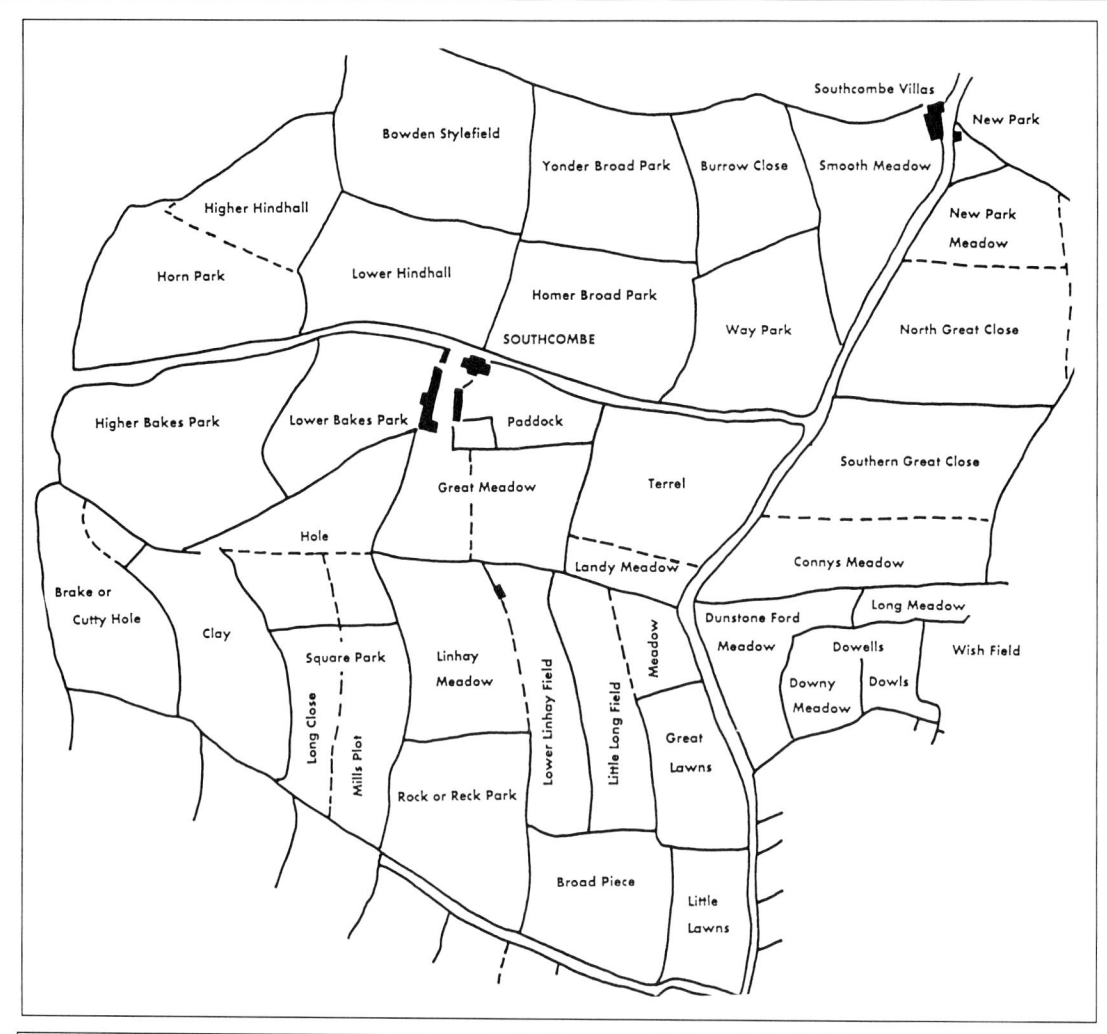

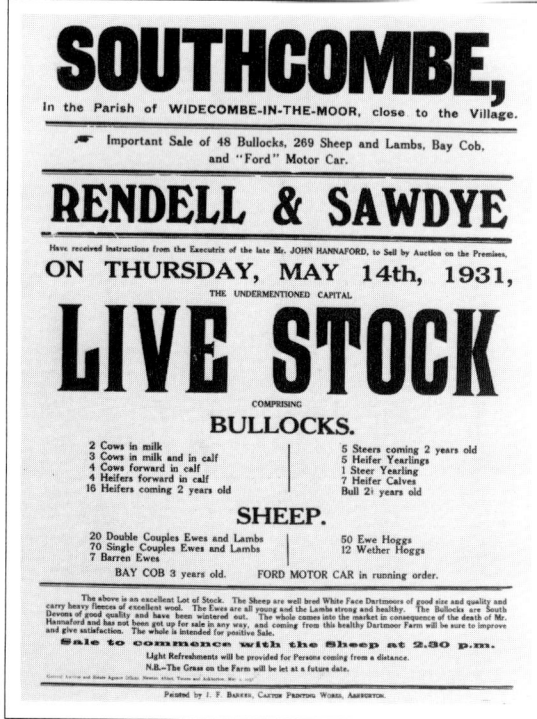

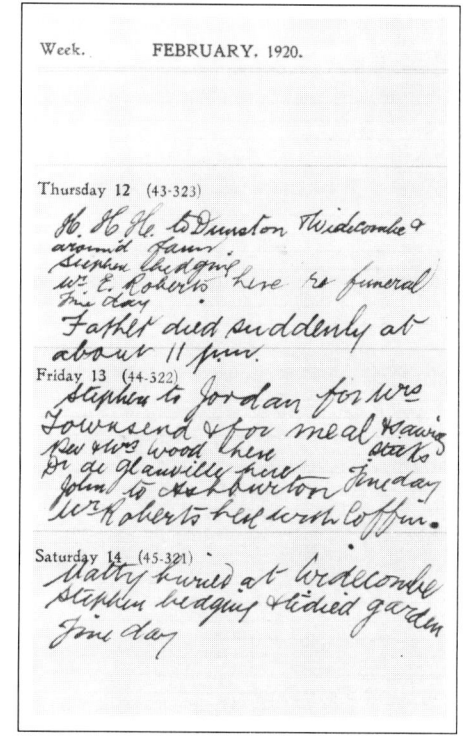

Top: layout and field names on Southcombe Farm. **Above left**: poster from 1931 advertising a livestock sale *(Hermon French)*. **Above right**: a page from the Southcombe diaries, 1920.

THE FARMYARD

Ponsworthy House farmyard - this photograph from c. 1900 provides a wonderful sense of the self-contained nature of farming in those days.

The roundhouse on Lizwell farm. This contained the mechanism powered by horses walking around a central shaft and driving machinery such as corn crushers on the farm.

HARVESTING

Left: haymaking. 1940s *(Iris Woods)*.

Below left: Veronica, Joan and Anthony Cave-Penny at Huccaby Farm, 1909. Mr Sollick (?) stands on the wain. *(Ronnie Cave-Penny)*.

Below: Jack Brown of Tremills stooking corn on Chittleford. *(Phyllis Pascoe)*.

William Mann on a hay rake at Ponsworthy Farm, 1930s. *(Marjorie and Geoff Weymouth)*.

THE FARMER AND HIS LABOURER

Above: John Hannaford and William Satterly heaving hay up into the loft at Southcombe Farm c. 1930. *(Deborah Hannaford)*.

Left: Richard and Edwin Turner cutting corn with scythes on Corndonford. *(Bessie French)*.

Below: Tom Hern, John Hannford, and Herbert Hern loading wheat on to a waggon. *(Deborah Hannaford)*.

Below left: Saving corn c. 1939; l-r Stan Norrish; Leonard Norrish; unknown; Richard Nosworthy. *(Barbara Norrish)*.

WIDECOMBE

Gathering ferns (bracken) for winter bedding c. 1930 - from a postcard by Chapman & Son. *(Iris Woods)*.

Harry Warren and William Mann with a dung cart. *(Marjorie and Geoff Weymouth)*.

THE FARMER AND HIS LABOURER

SHEEP

Ron Hill (left) and William Mann unloading sheep. Ron worked for Louis Prouse who had two one-ton Ford trucks. In 1941 they went to Plymouth to help clear rubble after the blitz. *(Marjorie and Geoff Weymouth).*

Of unique construction the sheepfold on the west flank of Stannon Tor was built by a Scots shepherd in the nineteenth century. He introduced Scotch sheep on to the moor.

WIDECOMBE

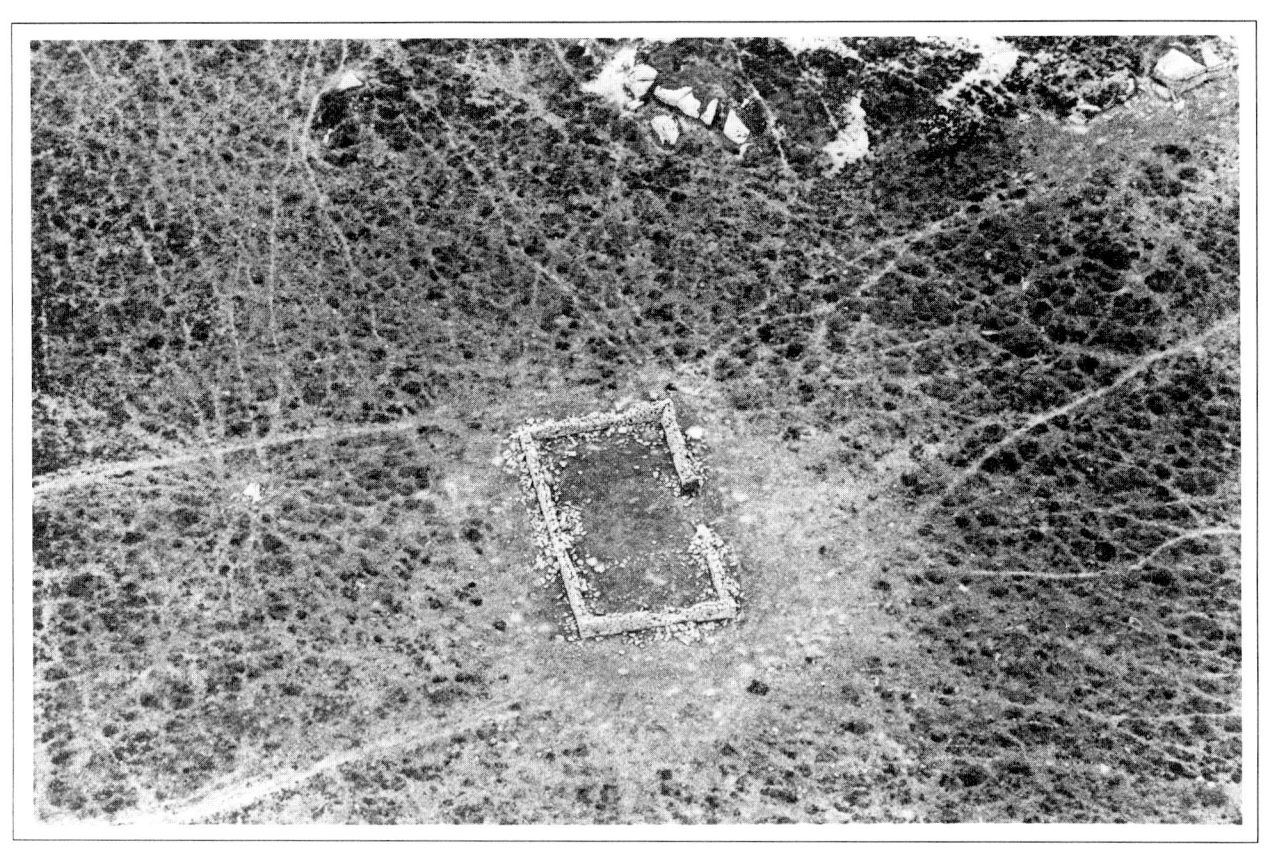

A sheepstell was an enclosure divided into pens each capable of holding a known number of sheep. This example lies under Laughter Tor and is associated with the 'gentry' farm of Brimpts whose owners would be likely to introduce such 'new' ideas into their farming in the nineteenth century.

Sydney Beard and Brag his dog, attending to a ewe and her twin lambs, in deep-lying snow on 28 February 1937. *(Sidney Beard).*

THE FARMER AND HIS LABOURER

A sheep shearing team (l-r) Bill Oldrieve, Sylvester Mann, Sam Cannon and Arthur Mann. With small flocks shearing was done by hand, even in the middle years of the present century. Powered clippers were later used widely and Arthur Mann, shown in these two photographs, is holding an electric clipper while the others hold 'dagging' shears - hand held spring shears. Wool from Dartmoor sheep was usually taken to Ashburton or Buckfastleigh for processing and use in the wollen mills there. *(Barbara Norrish)*.

The same team. Shearers took great pride in the speed and care they took in their work. *(Barbara Norrish)*.

THE MILK ROUND

Tony Beard, better known as 'The Wag from Widecombe' in his professional career as a comedian, is also a farmer at Bittleford Parks with his father Sidney Beard. He sent the following information concerning the distribution of milk supplies in the parish.

'In 1927 father started farming with two cows and their calves; the milk from the cows was used to feed the calves, supply family needs, while the surplus he sold to neighbouring cottagers.

It was customary at that time for farmers to supply their neighbours with milk, and this continued right up to the introduction of the 1947 Milk and Dairy Regulations Act.

This Act brought into being strict controls and conditions concerning the buildings in which milk could be produced, and the dairy where it was cooled and bottled, etc.

Many cow houses (shippons) had white-washed walls (painted with lime) and this all had to be scraped off and the walls smooth-rendered with cement, and all the floors had to be concreted and dung channels had to be provided, all with the aim of making the buildings easier to keep clean. This proved quite expensive, with the result that several farmers decided not to continue with milk production, and only those that brought their premises up to standard were issued with a license to produce and supply milk. Retail suppliers had particularly severe conditions to meet.

The majority of milk suppliers sent their milk to the factories (in this area it was Daws Creameries, later to become Unigate, at Totnes) where it was pasteurized or processed, and this is still the case today. But a few farmers were issued with Producer Retail Licences which permitted them to sell direct to the public. Father was one of these and there were others, among them Sweaton, Uphill, Venton, Southway, Glebe, Torr and Leightor. Eventually some of these gave up and the Bittleford Parks milk round gradually took them over.

As can be seen from this list there was a farm supplying each and every area of the parish. One of the first to give up was Sweaton who supplied all the houses in Ponsworthy 'east of the splash', and then Uphill who supplied the rest of Ponsworthy, and so we took them over. Then in, I believe, 1954 Southway gave up milking and they supplied all of Dunstone and Widecombe. The people of Dunstone asked us en bloc to supply them and we agreed, but the Totnes factory persuaded another person to deliver their milk in the village of Widecombe. This arrangement didn't last long and we were soon asked to supply the village, and this we did. We supplied most of the village with Mr Skinner of the Glebe supplying the rest.

I believe it was on Christmas Eve 1969 that we had several desperate telephone calls from the Poundsgate and Lowertown areas to say that they had been told that morning that the milk delivery was ceasing, and so we stepped in there to fulfil an urgent need. And so we continued until Novemeber 1984.

Two important developments took place in 1984 that completely altered the dairy scene. Firstly there was the introduction of quotas which restricted the amount of milk each producer could supply. At the same time more stringent controls over Producer Retailers came into force concerning the supply of untreated milk. Such milk could no longer be supplied to establishments that passed the milk on to a third party, i.e. shops, cafes, hotels and guest houses etc. The result of this was a drastic reduction in our rounds and on the 17 November 1984 we delivered our last pint of milk.'

The district now has its milk delivered from Ashburton.

In further correspondence Tony Beard says that before 1947 milk was supplied in jugs, enamel or tin cans with lids, pails or any other reasonable container. This was before bottles came into their own. 'I expect you can remember the cardboard disks that were set into the tops of the bottles, with a centre that you stuck your thumb into to pull it out. Then metal foil caps were to be used, coloured to depict various types of milk, plain silver for pasteurized, green for untreated, and gold for Channel Island. Cardboard containers were also used and you will remember our plastic sachets...'

The price of milk has risen over the years:

1944	7d per pint
1966	11d per pint
1976	10.5p per pint
1978	13.5p per pint
1982	20p per pint
1984	22p per pint

Tony Beard recalls: 'In the old days the milking herd was entirely the local South Devon breed. In 1953 we bought our first British Friesian and they have gradually become the dominant type, with a few Ayrshires, Guernseys and Jerseys and Redpolls.

THE FARMER AND HIS LABOURER

Farming scenes in the 1930s: Sidney Beard at Bittleford Parks. **Top**: hand milking; **centre left**: saving hay with a horse sweep; **centre right**: ploughing; **bottom**: Sydney and his son Anthony on a hay rake. *(Sydney Beard).*

THE WARRENER

'But as strange a thing as any of these was that concerning Robert Meade the Warriner; he being not missed all this while, immediately did Master Rouse his deare acquaintance remember him, and seeing him not, nor none knowing what was become of him, Master Rouse stepped to the window, looking into the Church where the Warriner used to sit, and there saw him sitting in his seate, leaning upon his elbow, his elbow resting upon the deske before him, he supposed him to be a sleepe, or aston'd, not yet come to himself; hee calling him to wake him, wondered hee made no answer, then his love to him caused him to venter into the Church, to jogg him awake, or to remember him, and then to his much griefe hee perceived his friend to bee a dead man; for all the hinder part of his head was cleane cut off and gone round about his neck and the forepart not disfigured, as supposed when they drew neare him.'

And so perished Richard Meade in the tornado which destroyed part of the church of Widecombe in 1638. He was 'warriner to Sir Richard Reynolds, his head was cloven, his skull rent in three places, and his braines thrown upon the ground whole, and the hair of his head, through the violence of the blow at first given him, did stick fast unto the pillar or wall of the church...'

Richard Meade is the first known warrener to have lived in Widecombe parish. Twenty-five years before his death the bounds of what was to become Vaghill Warren were set out in a deed between William, Earl of Bath, who owned Spitchwick Manor, and Richard Reynell and Walter Fursland.

The bounds lay in 'waste ground called Spitchwick common lying between the river Darte on the West and south east and from thence to Heator (Yar Tor) to Cornetor (Corndon Tor) on the north and east to the west of Rowbrook hedge and so to Logator (Lucky Tor) on the east and so to the river Darte with free liberty to make a warren there for the keeping breeding and killing of rabbits. And also if any rabbits go over the Darte to the common there called Holne Commons alias Holne Cleyves between Comson (Cumston) hedge and Whortaparke corner or to any place in the said Common of Spitchwick the said Richard and Walter may kill them. Rent 10/-.'

It was the task of the warrener to create ideal artificial homes (buries) for the rabbits, in which they would breed and grow as quickly as possible. The rabbits would then be killed for their meat and skins.

There are on the warren described above about 25 buries of varying length in addition to six vermin traps which were there to keep weasels and stoats away from the warren. One of these traps is of a type unique to Dartmoor. Beside the river is a stone-lined pit about 12 feet by 3 feet to which four funnel walls lead. It is said that the walls would lead any vermin towards the pit into which they would fall and drown.

It has been suggested that the ruins of two buildings at the head of Eazen Combe were 'warren houses' (where the warrener lived) but it is more likely they are ruins of workers' cottages. There is however a small ruined building just above the tree line and clitter that descends sharply to the banks of the Dart, and this is quite possibly a warren house. Just in front of the ruin is a small bury, a larger one a little farther off.

Though commercial warrens continued well into the present century their importance was already declining when William Crossing observed 'In the Great Blizzard of 1891 thousands of rabbits died on Dartmoor and the effect of the partial de-populaion of the warren is still felt.' Beside this primitive 'factory farming' of rabbits, the animals were always part of the diet of country people and hunting and snaring rabbits was a common pursuit.

The Southcombe diaries give a picture of the importance of catching rabbits, although how much of this was for the control of the pest, and how much a supplement to diet is difficult to assess. The diaries record that in 1919 there were 905 rabbits caught, being sold to 'Tonkin (359), Alford (333), Bennett (163), Snow (11), Symons (33) and Ashburton (6).' This raised a total of £58.0.11d.

A. Hearn was employed to trap rabbits but we see also that Stephen Hambley was set the task of catching rabbits presumably in order to meet specific market demands: 'August 11. Stephen trapping in Gt. Close.'

Hermon French went so far as to map the number of rabbits caught in the fields of two farms, Dockwell and East Shallowford in the 1950s. Whereas only a hundred or so were killed each year at Dockwell, more determined efforts at East Shallowford saw numbers caught in 1950 rising to nearly a thousand.

The advent of myxomatosis in 1955 decimated the rabbit population and this recurring disease keeps the numbers low compared to the past.

THE FARMER AND HIS LABOURER

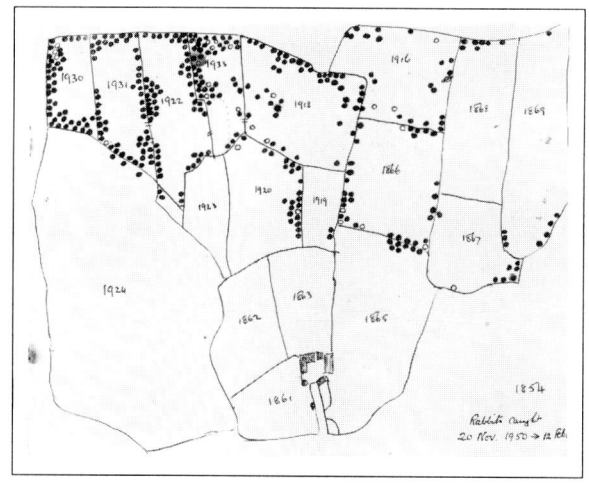

Top: An aerial view of Vaghill warren. The ruins of the warren house are centre left with the bury immediately behind. A large bury can be seen on the right.

Centre left and right: pages from Hermon French's notebook giving details of the numbers of rabbits caught in 1950 - and an amusing sketch 'Rabbits playing cowboys with snares, as seen by Pan Zab at East Shallowford, January 1951'. *(Hermon French).*

Left: The 'drowning pit' vermin trap at Vaghill Warren.

Clapper bridge over the West Webburn below Lower Cator.

TRANSPORT

The winding lanes criss-crossing the parish are based on early packhorse routes laid down in Saxon times. These negotiated the rivers and streams of Dartmoor at stepping stones, fordable crossings, or by simple clapper bridges and, later, more substantial packhorse bridges.

The clapper bridge was principally for foot traffic and it was wheeled traffic, farm waggons and coaches, that demanded better bridges be constructed. These had a less steep embankment and a high arch which gave plenty of room for rushing flood waters to pass through. Huccaby bridge is a fine example.

The whole evolution of river crossings can be seen at Postbridge. First the ford, a shallow stretch of water by the clapper bridge; then the stepping stones a hundred yards above the present road bridge; then the clapper bridge; and finally the eighteenth-century road bridge.

Dating bridges is difficult and it was not until 1888 that an Act made it a duty on public authorities to construct and maintain them. Until this time the responsibility fell on individual communities through the Waywardens, and earlier, on religious orders, to ensure that the highway and bridges were kept passable.

The Act made it the responsibility of the new County Council to maintain bridges and 300 feet of the highway at either side. In many places this is marked by a granite stone bearing the letter 'C' and these stones can still be found at Ponsworthy, Cockingford, Huccaby and Bellever, among others.

Following heavy rains and severe flooding in the spring of 1809 James Green, the County Surveyor, reported on a number of bridges that required immediate attention as 'being seriously injured by the late floods,' one of these being at Postbridge. 'I examined it and gave direction for the repair of the Piers and Foundation,' wrote Green, 'and for the forming of a weir with large granite stones below the bridge which will prevent the like damage in Future, and as the stones are there plentiful the expense will not exceed £20.'

This bridge was originally built by the Trustees of the Moretonhampstead Turnpike about 1772 but they were so neglectful that the County took it over around 1807. Seven other bridges in the parish were maintained by the County: Cockingford, Ponsworthy, Buckland, Newbridge and Dartmeet, Hexworthy and Bellever.

James Green's reports contain a number of adverse comments concerning the bridges of the parish and it is worth including two of these here, if only to illustrate the problems and pitfalls faced by travellers:

COCKMANFORD (Cockingford): Built with rough moor stone. Roadway 7ft 6ins, graveld. The west side of the road is not very good but the situation of the bridge being very remote it is perhaps good enough for its purpose.

PONSWORTHY: One very flat arch of 20ft span built with rough granite. Roadway 8ft wide and graveld; except some pointing and pinning up wanted in the parapets and one coping stone which is off, the whole is in tolerable order the situation being also rather private.

The author had to laugh on reading these comments for there has never been a time when this bridge did not require its coping stones to be reset. This bridge has won many a joust with car and coach and wears its battle scars royally.

Exactly how old the bridge is we do not know. It was reported to be in need of repair in 1664 and a stone here is dated 1666, with another repair date added in 1911.

A later bridge, that at Dartmeet, has a tablet stating 'County Bridge 1792'.

The Dymonds went there for a picnic on 28 September 1873. 'The spot where our dinner was spread at Dartmeet was near by the remains, still plainly visible, of the old clapper bridge, which Wm French remembers standing, and of which one of the clapper stones had been washed away in the flood in 1826.'

With the County taking on the care of larger bridges, the job of the Waywardens was made much easier but they still had to care for the numerous smaller bridges in the parish: Bonehill, Northway, Venton, Wooder, Dunstone, Bowdon, Stout, Shortcross, Wm. Stancombe's corner and Southcombeford being mentioned in the Combe Quarter accounts. In the Jordan Quarter, Shollaford, Watergate, Woodcock, and High appear. In the Spitchwick Quarter are Rex, Clerks, Blackaton and Forda; while only two appear in the Forest accounts, being Sherborn and O'Brook.

The Waywarden's accounts contain details of the costs relating to the upkeep of the highways and bridges in the parish. In 1783 they record that nine yards of new road were made between 'Dunstone Ford and Withecombe Town'. In 1837 'Pd. John Warren for building Dunstone Bridge £1. Pd. Joseph Leaman for drawing 4 large stone posts for Dunstone Bridge 10/-.'

Unusual items were also recorded. In the 1777 accounts for the Combe Quarter: 'Richard Pitcher for iron work for the clam or bridge 2/-' and in 1838 'John Smerdon's bill for railing Bunhill Bridge...'

The Waywardens were replaced by the Highway Boards towards the end of the last century and the Dymond Diaries on 26 July 1884 record: 'It should be mentioned on Thursday morning The Father met Mr Oliver the Surveyor of the Highway Board, in Dunstone Lane where the bridges that so long have been in a dangerous state are going to be repaired. In the process of time it is hoped the lane itself will be widened and improved but at present the Board appears to be in the state so often heard of when any new work is required "having laid out so much money lately, it can't do any new work".'

Repairs to roads and bridges were continuous as traffic increased. Gates too were of prime importance, stopping animals straying from the commons, and were considered as part of the highway. These were named Lizewell, Rowdon, Three Gates, Hackdown, Newgate, Greenaway, Streal, Oldsbrim Down, Pounds, Cator Down, Pepper Lane, Grendon Down, Huston, Lower Stout, Blendiwell, Bonehill Down, Bowdon Down and Ludgate.

The author remembers that as a small boy he was quite envious of the Rowden 'boys' as they seemed to be sitting on a gold mine and spent endless hours opening their gate and collecting pennies from grateful drivers. Most of the gates have now decayed, their posts removed for road widening, being replaced by cattle grids.

Little known packhorse bridge across the East Webburn on a track from Buckland to Ponsworthy.

TRANSPORT

Top: Dartmeet clapper bridge, destroyed in a storm in 1826.

Centre left: dated stone recording repairs made to Ponsworthy bridge in 1666 and 1911.

Centre: '1 miol' stone on the road to Natsworthy. In his book *Boundary Markers On and Around Dartmoor*, Dave Brewer suggests this might have served as a parole stone, marking the limit to which prisoners of war on parole could progress.

Centre right: a cross cut on a gatepost at the lower end of the track to Kingshead. This may have been a waymark along the church path to Pizwell.

Left: Huccaby pack horse bridge over the West Dart.

WAYWARDENS

The first Act of Parliament to control the maintenance of roads was passed in 1555 and not materially altered until 1835, a period of 280 years. At Widecombe five volumes of highway accounts have survived, though some are unfortunately missing. They begin in 1769 and continue until 1864 with the missing years being 1809-1838, and 1847-1856.

Because of its size the parish was divided into four Quarters. These were Coombe (or Combe), Dewdon, Spitchwick and the Forest Quarter, this latter being outside the parish proper. Within this area the Waywardens, elected by the parish, were responsible for the upkeep of roads and bridges.

Under the Act of 1555 everyone having an annual rate of £50, plus those keeping draught horses or plough, had to provide one wain or cart with oxen, horses or cattle, and two able men. Every male householder, cottager and labourer had to go himself or send one sufficient labourer in his place for six consecutive days' work of eight hours each per annum. On the poor labourer whose wages were just above subsistence this imposed a severe strain.

Among the Waywarden's duties were those of viewing all roads, highways, watercourses and bridges three time a year. He had to see that the owners of land adjacent to the highway kept ditches clear and trees and bushes lopped, and the highway free from obstruction.

On the Sunday following each inspection the Waywarden was required to stand in the church and proclaim all the faults he had discovered. Doing so he would announce the dates of the six day's labour to the congregation. Being absent from church was not considered an excuse for defaulting, all such being reported to the Justices.

An Act of 1563 gave the Justices of the Peace the powers to indict those responsible if the highways fell into disrepair, fining them sufficiently to cover the costs of repair. This fine was passed on to the Waywardens to see that the work was undertaken.

Such justice had its effects on the statutory labour laws. Why should one labourer do his statutory duty only to be fined when another defaulted. This contributed to the unpopularity of the laws and it became quite commonplace for the parish to find itself regularly indicted for neglect. Examples of this can be seen by comparing cases in the Quarter Sessions with the Waywardens' accounts:

Quarter Sessions - Widecombe-in the-Moor:
Midsummer 1776 - the road in length 40 perch and in breadth 6ft. called Sweadon Lane. Epiphany 1777 - Transversed. Easter 1777 - Defendant acquitted.

Waywardens' accounts:
1780. Expended for myself and horse in going to Newton to receive the fine which had been paid by order of the Justices.

Quarter Sessions:
Epiphany 1792 - The road in length 2 miles in breadth 8ft. from Ponsworthy Village in the p'sh of Withecombe to Lox Gate and from there to Dartmeet Bridge. Witness Joseph Sanders. Midsummer 1792 - Discharged on oath of prosecution.

Waywardens' accounts:
1792 - for taking the indictment £2.16.0.

And so the Waywardens collected monies imposed as fines by the magistrates in order to then pay for road repairs. The main problem with this was that the Waywardens were elected for a year only and thus had little experience or incentive to prosecute their duties. Similarly the labourer had little experience in roadmending techniques and almost no incentive to carry them out.

The usual method of maintenance was to take a cartload of stone and empty it into the worst potholes, allowing the traffic to settle it in. Basic tools were provided by the parish, pick axe, sledge and bar-iron - later a wheelbarrow. It is noticeable that shovels and spades were not included - the labourer supplying his own.

There were those who should have provided transport but did extra labour instead: '1769. Silvester Mann 12 days in lieu of horse and cart.' The work could be arduous, as Beatrice Chase describes: 'It is not the weight of the hammer which is trying, many tools used by the workmen are heavier. It is the ceaseless jar of the metal on the granite which runs like electric stabs of pain all up the nerves and muscles of the arms. The young roadmender cannot sleep at night for the agony, his arms feel drawn and shrunken.'

The use of wheeled vehicles on Dartmoor was rare until the present century and there are still those who remember Old Granny Caunter of Ponsworthy who would not allow a wheeled cart on her farm for she claimed it ruined the gateways.

TRANSPORT

Above left: a typical page from the Waywardens' accounts, October 1775–October 1776.

Above: a postcard by Beatrice Chase showing roadmenders at work. In the foreground is George Ford, one of Beatrice Chase's 'Bluejackets', the other man is Bill Beard. *(Gwen Beard).*

Left: Jack Warren, foreman roadmender, outside Uppacot cottage. *(Barbara Norrish).*

White Gate c. 1930 - from a postcard by Chapman & Sons. The modern road has been widened and the gate replaced by a cattle grid. *(Iris Woods).*

The author with his brother, John Woods, viewing the damage done to the road above Bonehill by the great storm of 1938. *(Iris Woods).*

Iris Woods, the author's mother, sits at the edge of the storm-damaged road just below Bonehill Farm, 1938. *(Iris Woods).*

HORSE-DRAWN TRANSPORT

The Dymond Diaries contain many references to the use of the horse and carriage including 'The Father' leaving every monday morning to return to his work as a solicitor, or to carry out his magisterial duties.

A preoccupation with the state of the roads comes through clearly and it is significant that the present road from White Gate down to Bovey Tracey is always referred to as just a path.

Mr Joll of Bovey Tracey did most of the family's carriage work but his life was not without problems. On 9 November 1871 the family was returning to Exeter after five months at Blackslade: 'as if to make the moorland experience complete just as we were crossing the moorland stream Carrie jumped completely into a bog and felt herself gradually sinking nearly up to her waist in 'slushy' mud, no pleasant sensation it must be confessed especially when it was found that the ground all round was so soft that it seemed impossible to get her out.

Mr Joll was a friend in need and by a strong pull and a great struggle Carrie was tugged out very wet but fortunately not too much chilled for a hot fire and a 'cup of tea' at the Dolphin to warm through again.'

Carrie had other, less trying, excursions through the parish. In August 1894 for instance: 'The Mother [Carrie Tosswill] with the little girls and the babies have found pleasures and occupations nearer home and pleasant expeditions in William Beard's carriage to Spitchwick and Dartmeet have been made.'

The author's mother was also among these early summer visitors to Widecombe and wrote:

'As a small child it was the long summer holiday that was the highlight of the year. My parents and I lived in Middlesex and when the summer term ended I was sent down to my grandparents in Exeter, and it was from here that the great expedition set out, my grandparents, 3 aunts, the cook and the house parlour maid in a two horse waggonette. With us went a whole ham, a whole cheddar cheese, 2 tins of biscuits (one sweet, one plain) some essential groceries and the family's cat in a basketwork hamper.

Chudleigh to rest the horses, with milk and buns at the bakers - then on again. I can still remember my pride when considered old enough to walk up the hill out of Bovey Tracey. The sight of the village deep below us from the top of Widecombe Hill, a thrilling moment, though a little nervous of the horses slipping, which they never did.

Our first cottage was outside the village but later we had a lease of a house we named Wayside [now the Wayside Cafe]. Until the early 1920s my grandmother used to sit in the front garden watching the passerby and remarking with satisfaction "There'll never be motor cars here" when a vehicle failed to negotiate the steep hill up to the Green.

This reminds me of a story one of my childhood friends in Widecombe told me recently. In 1909 the then Prince and Princess of Wales made a brief stop in the village on their way to Huccaby races. They came in a car and my friend, aged 12, rushed into her mother begging her to come out and see them and the motor car - to which her mother replied "I've seen a motor car" and went on with her baking.

The village green was a play place for us children and there is still a large sycamore where we hid our toys away in its gnarled roots when other mothers called us to dinner. We never had cause to doubt that they would still be safe when we returned. Now and then on fine days during the summer a [horse-drawn] charabanc visited the village. The first hint of its arrival was the sound of a horn as it slowly descended Widecombe Hill - but with what a clatter it arrived in the village as the horses were urged up the last little pinch at top speed.'

In her book *Dartmoor and Its Surroundings* published in 1900, Beatrice F. Cresswell provides another decription of a coach trip on Dartmoor. One trip was from Bovey Tracey to Widecombe, Cator Court, Grimspound and back by Manaton, a round trip of 30 miles:

I counsel the nervous to insist upon walking down Widdecombe Hill, for a more fearful descent to drive down on the top of a coach cannot well be imagined, one expects to be overturned every moment; the horses ears look to be below us, and the bottom of the descent is nowhere visible. [The coach had three brakes and a ship's rope lashed around the wheels].

It is a wonderful bit of work for the horses and one is glad to know that as soon as they get in they have a mash with a bottle of gin in it: the drivers at the Dolphin having tried many pick-me-ups for the teams after this tremendous effort, and finding gin best of all!'

WIDECOMBE

This wonderful picture captures the importance of horse-drawn vehicles prior to the arrival of motorised transport. Moving house from Stone to Natsworthy c. 1906, the horse is being fed prior to setting off with a flat-bed farm waggon with an extraordinary load. *(Iris Woods)*.

TRANSPORT

THE CAR

'July 30th 1920: Car arrived.' This note in the Southcombe Diaries heralded the arrival of (possibly) the first privately owned motor car in the parish. It did not have an auspicious beginning for within a week 'car back to Moreton and broken again,' and the following day 'car to Ilsington and Bulpin's men here mended car.'

With the arrival of the car Cecil Churchward also came into his own, driving, maintaining and painting the vehicle when he was not engaged in general work on the farm. This was to be his job for the next ten years when, as Jack Prouse recalls, 'Cecil and his wife moved to Ashburton and opened a greengrocery business.'

Having got the car, the open road beckoned the Hannafords and, of course, friends and family were not forgotten: 'Monday 23rd August Mr and Mrs J.S.H. to Grimspound, Vicarage Throwleigh and Dunston,' and on the following day 'Mr and Mrs J.S.H. to Dockwell, New House, Postbridge, Princetown, Dartmeet.'.

Sidney Beard, remembers when John Hannaford first got a car: 'they loaded up five or six of the children at a time and took them on a round trip via Venton, Dunstone and back to Widecombe.'

The diaries also note 'car crashed' on a number of occasions!

Tony Beard recorded his father's memories of these early vehicles:

'Another car in the district belonged to the Radcliffes of Bag Park, who also owned the Old Inn and Glebe Farm. It was they who built the garage facing the Green for their car, which is now "the Shop on the Green". Jim Courtier was their chauffeur and one day when driving up the valley towards Bag Park he had just crossed Wooder Bridge when the car caught fire and burnt out.

The Revd Wood also had a Morgan three-wheeler and my father can remember sitting on the back of it and having a ride. He also remembers that there were times when the Revd Wood came out of the Vicarage yard and turned too quickly and tipped over.

Of course there were a fair amount of mishaps, he remembers Nurse Horton who had a Baby Austin 7 tourer in the late 1920s. She was with Mary Hambley one day and tipped the car over up Eastern Lane (what we tend to call Easter Lane), and Father was working in our yard when they came in to ask for help. So he went and helped them tip it up onto its wheels and off they went again.

Earnest Beard did his grocery rounds around the parish for years, firstly by horse and trap and carriage, but in the mid 1920s he bought a Ford 1-ton van, replacing it with a Chevrolet in the 1930s. He had seats made to fit inside the van and used it on Wednesdays (market day) to go to Newton to collect his stock for the shop, and as a bus for the locals.

I can remember doing the rounds with him, having all the groceries in the back and in the middle carrying five-gallon drums of paraffin, the main cooking and heating fuel of the time.

Father thinks that Bill Miners was possibly the first to transport cattle to market. He also had a Ford 1-ton truck and he fixed some sides to it and a tailgate but it did not have a loading ramp.

He thinks that the first cow and calf taken to market in this way belonged to Farmer Mann at Lizwell and they brought the animals up to Bittleford and backed the lorry against the high bank and drove them into the lorry from there. When they got to market there was a concrete ramp to back up against for unloading. Louis Prouse of Ponsworthy also had a 1-ton truck and Ron Hill was his assistant.

Commander Jones, who lived at Windwhistle, owned Bittleford Farm and Jordan Farm (The Manor), along with ground at Bittleford Parks and Old Walls. In the early twenties he had an International tractor which must have been one of the first in the area.

One little story you may find amusing about transport in those days: Father had been up to Bonehill to see his Uncle Jim, James Beard, the postman and farmer, and was riding his bicycle home, came down Bonehill Lane and shot out at the bottom of Widecombe Hill and went right under a car which was coming from Widecombe. The driver was so upset he immediately gave Father 25/- for a new front wheel.'

The car eventually gave access to millions of visitors to Widecombe, killing off the local bus service, for almost every family came to own a car. Tractors and mechanical equipment now abounds on the farms, and man-made tors of granite boulders spring up at the edges of fields as the larger stones are cleared so easily from the land.

WIDECOMBE

The visit of the Prince and Princess of Wales (later to become King George V and Queen Mary) to Huccaby races in 1909 caused a great stir among the people of Widecombe, indeed the whole of Dartmoor. The royal party arrived in the westcountry by train and processed by car across the moor to Huccaby, via Widecombe. This photograph shows the considerable crowd outside the Church House eagerly awaiting their arrival. Percy Prouse can be seen at the front of the group, a small boy in a tweed jacket and cap, standing with his hands in his pockets. *(May Hambley)*.

HUCCABY RACES

Regular meetings were held at the moorland race-course but on the day of the royal visit the crowds were exceptionally large and the bookies did a roaring trade. *(Jack Prouse)*.

TRANSPORT

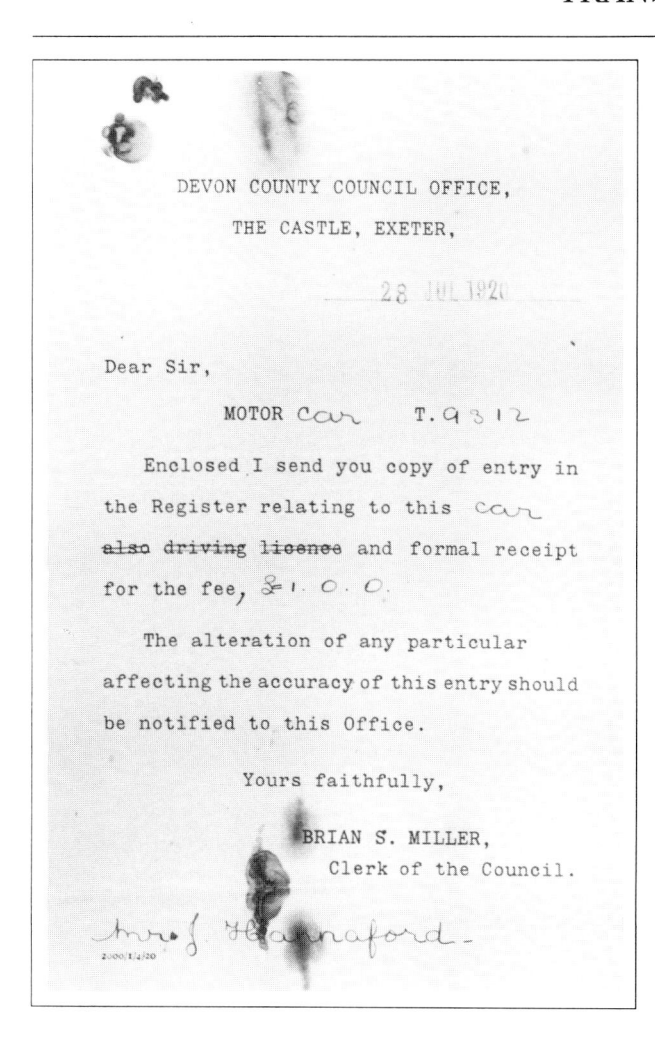

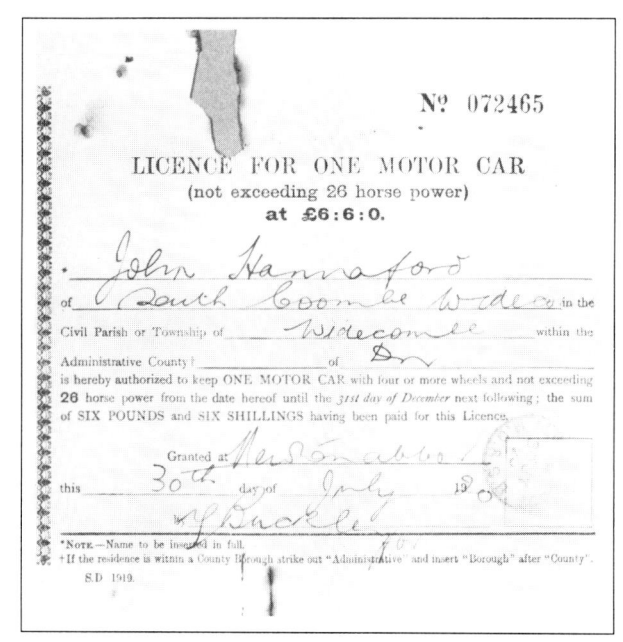

Above left: the registration document of John Hannaford's model T Ford. *(Hermon French)*.

Above: the annual licence for the car cost £6.6s in 1920, not a small sum even then. *(Hermon French)*.

Below: just sixteen years after the arrival of John Hannaford's car the village was beginning to get a glimpse of current traffic problems. This photograph was taken at Widecombe Fair in 1936. Note Wilfred Beard's cattle truck on the right. *(Annie Main)*.

THE RURAL BUS SERVICE

I am indebted to Gwen Beard for the following history of local transport:

Widecombe-in-the-Moor Transport 1900-1971

Widecombe Parish had public transport from early 1900 carried on by the Beard family. Ernest Beard who was a general dealer and shopkeeper at Linchaford, Ponsworthy, also plied for public hire with horse and cariage, or waggonette.

Visitors came to Dartmoor for their holidays even in those days. The only way to get to their destination was by horse transport. Ernest led a busy life with help, especially in the summer months, meeting passengers from various GWR stations, Bovey Tracey, Moretonhampstead, Ashburton and Newton Abbot, conveying them to their respective guest-houses on the moor. This also meant transporting them back to the stations at the end of the holiday.

Ernest (who became my father-in-law) had two sons, Wilfred, who became my husband, and Sidney. When the boys were growing up both helped their father in the business, all sharing a great love of horses.

In 1923 when Wilfred was seventeen years old his father considered the age of the motor car had arrived and sent him to Bulpin's garage at Newton Abbot to learn to drive a car and how to maintain it mechanically. This accomplished his father purchased a new Model T Ford and this started motor car transport in Widecombe.

Having bought the car Wilfred's father told him to take it out on private hire and, when he had earned enough money to pay his father for it, the car was his to start his own business with. This he did.

Visitors came to Dartmoor and the car for hire was in great demand by visitors, and also by parishioners. After a period of private hire Wilfred decided to operate a kind of bus service from Ponsworthy to Ashburton on Saturday mornings, the limit being four seats. This proved very successful though, with this and private hire, he could not accommodate all the passengers. Consequently he bought a second car, a Paige Jowett, a little larger than the Ford.

By this time his brother Sidney had also taught himself to drive and the two brothers operated both cars for several years on this small but efficient route. In 1931 Wilfred built his own garage and accommodation at Church Lane Head, about one mile from the centre of Widecombe village, and he began to operate from there.

About 1934 the bus era had started all over the country. The government decided to set up licencing authorities to control the operation of bus companies. Our local authority operated from Bristol covering the whole of the West Country.

Although our enterprise was small we had to register but were not subject to regulations as our vehicles had less than six seats. At this time one or two other people with a private car started to operate a bus service with a car over our route. Although this did not affect us passenger-wise they were a nuisance, opposing everything we did.

In about 1936 Devon County Council invited tenders for a 14-seater coach to transport senior children from Widecombe School to Ashburton school daily. After some consideration Wilfred submitted a tender for this operation and was successful. Now the problem arose as how to find a suitable vehicle for the job, especially as Ponsworthy Bridge had a restriction on it as to size and weight.

Eventually he found a 14-seater Chevrolet coach and this was used to transport children to Ashburton after they had reached 11 years of age. On Saturdays the bus was used for regular services working under a published timetable.

By this time we had to employ one driver, though Sidney, who also worked as a farmer, helped when he could.

In 1937 we were successful in submitting a tender to carry schoolchildren from outlying districts into Widecombe school and the search began for another 14-seater coach. Once in operation we collected children from as far away as Challacombe and Natsworthy.

We wanted to use the second bus also on a Saturday run but we were opposed in this by Devon General and by Potters of Haytor. In the end we were obliged to work out our own route and have our own bus tickets printed, and hire a ticket punch. We were also able to operate a service from Ashburton to Widecombe.

Wilfred now took over the Wednesday Market bus. By law a notice had to be displayed inside the coach No livestock to be carried. At each stop the driver would be asked if he could put parcels in the boot, very carefully tied small sacks, carefully camouflaged cardboard boxes with live chickens, braces of rabbits, and on occasion a live goose.

In 1963 sadly Wilfred died and I carried on the until April that year when our son David came into the business thus becoming the third generation of Beards to operate transport in Widecombe parish. We carried on until 1971 when I retired and we sold the business.

My biggest heartache was selling the two little Chevrolet buses which had given excellent service and carried thousands of passengers over the years.

TRANSPORT

Beard's Garage 1950s, l-r: Bob Palmer; Fred Bamsey; Wilfred Beard; Gwen Beard; Michael Nosworthy; Jim Hine. *(Gwen Beard)*.

Wilfred Beard clearing snow outside his garage, 1960s. *(Gwen Beard)*.

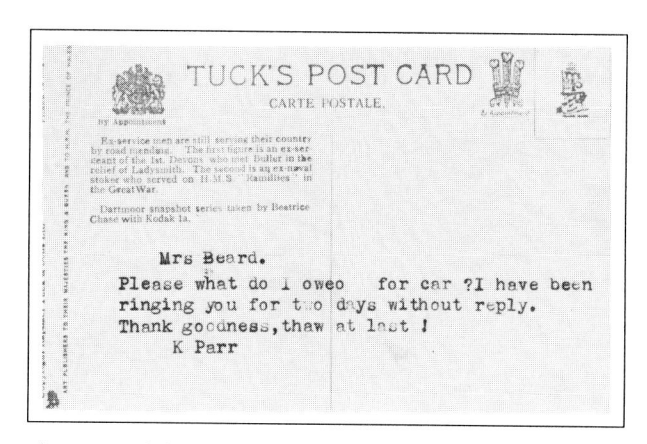

A postcard from Katharine Parr (on a Beatrice Chase postcard) to Mrs Beard. *(Gwen Beard)*.

WIDECOMBE

Dartmoor ponies grazing on the village green.

Above: The Cross Tree.

Right: the stone commemorating the coronation of King George VI stands at the base of a copper beech planted on the green on that occasion.

THE VILLAGE GREEN

John Hooker writes of Devonshire people 'Notwithstanding they be both of a mighty and strong bodye, hable to endure all laboures and tymes of leasure they do geve thym selves unto such exercises and pasttymes as where wth they do rather inseme theire bodyes wth hardness and strength, then otherwyse As wth shotynge wrastelynge and hurlynge.'

Countless thousands of visitors walk on the village green at Widecombe each year, how many know that its old name was Butts Park. This name derives from its ancient use as an area of land set aside for archery practice. This came from an edict of Edward II who directed that 'every Englishman should have a bow of his own height, of yew, ash, wych hazel or amburn, and that butts should be made in every township, which the inhabitants were to shoot at every feast-day under penalty of a halfpenny when they should omit that exercise.'

Two other manors in Widecombe parish, Jordan and Spitchwick also have fields with names that denote this former usage: Butts Field in Bittleford and Butts Ware on Lower Uppacot.

There is evidence of another use for the green for in the account of the Great Storm of 1638 we read: 'There was a bowling alley neare unto the churchyard, which was turned up into pits and heaps, a manner as if it had been plowed.' The green is nearest to the north-east side of the tower which was damaged by the tornado.

The old name for bowling was 'kales' or 'keels' (hence the expression 'to keel over'), and the most famous westcountry exponent was, of course, Sir Francis Drake. Writing in her *Borders of the Tamar and Tavy* in the last century Mrs Bray relates 'This is our provincial name for what, I believe, is nothing more than the common game of nine-pins of skittles, now played by the vulgar in public house yards.'

As Hooker describes, wrestling was another popular sport in Devon, and Baring-Gould writes of William Thorne the renowned Widecombe wrestler. There is no documentary evidence for wrestling on the green but it is quite likely. It was certainly the place where Widecombe Fair was first held.

The green is also to be noted for some fine trees. The author's mother decribes the splendid old sycamore that she played beneath in her childhood (see page 135), one of a number of trees holding a special place in parish history.

When the newell stairs were re-opened in the church, three crosses were found. These now stand against the pillar at the rear of the church. An octagonal shaft of another cross, along with a broken head taken from the churchyard wall, was re-erected inside the south entrance. This cross originally stood on a base in the village square, but that position was usurped by a yew tree, known as the Cross Tree.

There is a note in the parish records 'in February 1795 a yew tree from the vicarage garden was planted on the cross' and written in another hand 'which died in 1860 and a young one planted in its place.' The description 'on the cross' here refers to the granite plinth on which the yew tree still grows. It is likely that, in accordance with tradition, a yew tree has been grown here for centuries.

On 2 December 1822 an elm tree from the Vicarage garden was planted in the trunk of an old elm which at its base measured 18 feet around. Sadly this tree died during the Dutch Elm Disease epidemic and was cut down in 1978.

The Churchwardens' accounts also refer to particular 'parish trees'. In 1860 it was recorded that 'the churchwardens do have custody of Two Parish Trees - Elm and Yew, and are held responsible for proper care of the same, and that wood cut off be stored away for use of the School board.'

The elm is probably the tree mentioned in 1736: 'it is agreed that whatsoever Ffoxes are Taken or killed within the Parish are to be brought to the Church Town and hung up in the Parish Tree... there shall be paid 5 shillings for every fox and vixen that are able to prey for themselves, and to take money out of the Poor Rates.'

The Churchwardens also put a bounty on the head of other animals and birds: Greys (badgers) 1 shilling; Mattron (pine martens) 3d; Hedgehog 3d. Pollcat 3d; Weasel 3d; Kite 2d; Jay 1d; Hoop (bullfinch) 1/2d. In 1719 they paid for 'killing 4 otters and a wild cat.'

'On Tuesday June 21st 1887 a young oak tree was planted in the churchyard on the North side, about twenty paces from the back wall of the vestry. Weather and season both very unfavourable for planting. If it grows however it is to go by the name of the "Jubilee Oak."' The name lapsed but the tree survived and grew into a splendid specimen - sadly lately cut down - leaving the north side bare.

A lovely copper beech was planted to commemorate the coronation of George VI and has a stone engraved GR VI 1937 at its base. A small metal plaque acknowledges the planting of a tree in 1953 to celebrate the present queen's coronation.

WIDECOMBE

Uncle Tom Cobley (Ned Dunn), the spirit of Widecombe Fair, salutes at the original village sign - from a postcard by Valentine & Sons c. 1930. *(Iris Woods)*.

WIDECOMBE FAIR

In the Parish Register for Marriages 1813-1837 is to be found a very interesting memorandum written on the flyleaf at the back of the book: 'Widecombe in the Moor, 25th October, 1850. We the undersigned were present at the first Fair this day established in this village and dined with the Revd H. Mason, at the Vicarage House to celebrate the same as a Free Fare.

John Tozer for Solomon Tozer agent for the Rev. T. Fry, Lord of the Manor of Widecombe. Thomas Estcourt - Creswell. Jno. German Morton, Chairman, James Woodley, Halsehaage - bought 34 sheep. John Sparke Amay, Druid, Ashburton. Robt Nosworthy - Ford, Manaton. Henry Hals Scagell, Farmer. John May, Yeoman, Moretonhampstead. W.B. German, Yeoman, Moreton. John Pearce, Butcher, Ashburton. John Coaker, Yeoman, Bellaford.'

Little did they know that, through the imaginings of one man, their sheep fair was to become nationally and internationally famous, and that thousands upon thousands of visitors would crowd the lanes on the second Tuesday in each September; thus belying the chorus sung by the girls of Widecombe school 'Widecombe Fair -nobody there!'

There were certainly times when few turned up. The author's grandfather the Revd Leonard McCrea could remember that on one fair day the weather was so bad that only one sheep was tethered on the green. The Southcombe Diaries also record, in 1922 'Southerly storm in the afternoon - spoilt the Widecombe Fair sports.'

The Revd Sabine Baring-Gould collected folk song of the westcountry and one ballad, *Widecombe Fair*, became instantly famous when it was published. He embroidered the story by suggesting that the original character was one Thomas Cobley who lived in a house near Yeoford junction in the parish of Spreyton. He declared his will was signed on 20 January 1787 and proved on 14 March 1794.

It was as though Baring-Gould had opened a Pandora's box for it was later found that this Tom Cobley was a red-headed batchelor and that there was a proliferation of red-headed children in the Spreyton area. The names of his companions in the song were found in the registers of Sticklepath - and so the legend grew.

The author's grandfather broadcast on radio in 1947, relating the story of Widecombe Fair and singing the song. Tony Beard, 'The Wag from Widecombe' once sang it on television watched by the author 150 miles away - and all this when Tom Cobley died more than fifty years before the first fair was held!

No mention of the fair appears in any of the parish records until 1850, when it is recorded: 'Labour in Fair Park 1/6. Printing bills for the Fair 5/-.'

In the first few decades of the present century, as more and more visitors came to Widecombe, the villagers took it upon themselves to provide the visitors with what they wanted. On each fair day Edward Dunn of Dunstone put on a smock and paraded with a grey mare with local children riding it sporting cotton wool beards. The Kernicks got hold of a copy of the will and had it printed, selling them in their hundreds. Florence Prowse (née Kernick) wrote a small book about the village, calling herself 'a Moor-bred Native'. On the back of this booklet was a handwritten copy of Uncle Tom's goods and chattels. There was also printed a coloured broadsheet depicting the 'Cobley' story, while Ned Dunn and friends went out on the moor to have their photographs taken for a series of postcards.

The part of Uncle Tom Cobley is still played by local characters at each fair, a part taken by Peter Hicks for many years, following a long and proud tradition.

The sports have been a popular part of fair day for many years although the 1924 programme makes no mention of the famous Uncle Tom Cobley race. The author remembers that in the 1940s the contestants were herded into cattle trucks and taken to the top of the hill from whence they would race to the finish line in the Fair Field. In early years any one of a number of fields was used but in recent times it has always been the same field. Other events have included pillow fights, morris dancing, tug of war and a gymkhana.

But the main purpose of the day was originally as a sheep fair and this remains a major part of events today. The Southcombe Diaries contain regular entries relating to the numbers of ewes and rams sold. Other stock, including ponies, was taken along to the fair, both to be sold and to be entered into competition.

And so the tradition continues. Today the fair annually attracts thousands of visitors just as it has done for well over a hundred years. An entry in the Dymond Diaries for 12 September 1871: 'Today is Widecombe Fair and all the world has been thither to disport itself and to transact its business.'

WIDECOMBE

WIDECOMBE FAIR

Is one of the most famous traditional songs of all time, although other parts of the country claim the tune, the words are forever Widecombe's. Part of the annual fair, held on the second Tuesday in September, includes the re-enactment of the last journey of Tom Cobley's white mare, with the various parts being played by local volunteers. This series of postcards by E. Scott of Ashburton date from the 1930s. *(Iris Woods).*

Tom Pearce, Tom pearce, lend me your Grey Mare,
All along, down along, out along lee;
For I want to go to Widdecombe Fair,
With Bill Brewer, Jan Stewer, Peter Gurney,
Peter Davy, Dan'l Whiddon, Harry Hawk,
Old Uncle Tom Cobley and all!
Old Uncle Tom Cobley and all!

PHOTO 1
"Borrowing the Grey Mare"
left to right: Arthur Brown, Bill Brown (father of Arthur), Marjorie Brown (daughter), Annie Brown (wife of Bill), Ned Dunn.

PHOTO 2
"Tom Pearse he sat on a stone and he cried"
left to right: Bill Brown, Kenneth Brown, Stanley Brown, Arthur Brown, Bert Dunn (Ned's son), Ned Dunn.

PHOTO 3
"Her rattling bones"
clockwise from left: Ned Dunn, Bill Brown, Stanley Brown; Annie Brown, Kenneth Brown, Jackie Piper, Nick Soper.

PHOTO 4
"Tom Pearce's Mare appears ghastly white"
left to right: Arthur Brown, Kenneth Brown, Jack Piper, Bill Brown, Ned Dunn (without hat), Annie Brown, Stanley Brown, Nick Soper.

WIDECOMBE FAIR

Widecombe Fair c. 1905. *(Ena Prowse)*.

Postcard with a postmark dated 1906.

Above: Tom Hext of Ponsworthy and Uncle John Hannaford of Headland at Widecombe Fair c. 1940. *(Tony Beard)*.

Left: Widecombe Fair, mid 1930s. *(Iris Woods)*.

WIDECOMBE

Above left: Widecombe Fair, sheep judging 1936. *(F. Main)*.

Above: police constable on traffic duty at the Fair, 1936. *(Annie Main)*.

Left: Widecombe Fair c. 1932, l-r (on the horse): Jack Prouse, Jack Vincent, Jack Lawrence, Bob Lawrence, Raymond Warren, Edward (Ned) Dunn (standing with arm raised); Bob Hitchcock (in cap behind Ned Dunn) - Beatrice Chase described one of her Bluejackets as 'the faithful Hitchcock.' *(Jack Prouse)*.

Below: Tom Cobley (Peter Hicks) at Widecombe Fair in the 1990s.

SPORTING LIFE AND LEISURE

Hunting has always been a part of Dartmoor life, from the time of the Normans when they held it as a Royal Forest. The present South Devon Hunt frequently meet in the parish. This hunt was established by the famous George Templer - a great eccentric who is also remembered for his opening of the Haytor quarries and the building of the granite tramway there. When Templer hunted his pet monkey went along too, strapped on a horse.

The Dymond Diaries for 6 October 1884 record: 'The drive was made very interesting by the sight of the huntsmen and Whidbourne's hounds in full cry after a fox on Chittleford Newtake, which was finally killed in the hollow between Blackslade Ford and the Ashburton Road.'

Templer was just one of numerous 'characters' involved in the hunting scene. Freda Wilkinson relates how Tom French, baptised in Widecombe in 1781, 'was very fond of hunting and always went out on a white donkey and never had a horse, he wore a red coat given to him by the master, Sir Henry Seale of Holne Cot where the hounds were kept. The kennels are there now.'

Freda also remembers Ned Chapman, as does Jack Prouse, who lived at Buckland for many years.

It was not just the fox that was hunted. The Dymond Diaries tell us that Dartmoor Hunting week began on 1st May 1876 and on the following day they rode up onto the moor above Natsworthy to watch the Harriers chasing a hare on Himildon.' Other sports and pastimes included tug of war and the usual games and sports that accompanied Widecombe Fair each year. Another favourite pastime was Morris Dancing with both men's and women's teams being strongly represented in the 1930s and 1940s.

The South Devon Hunt - Sam Cannon on the grey horse at far left. *(Barbara Norrish).*

WIDECOMBE

Hunt meeting outside the Church House - hunstman Ned Chapman facing the camera. *(Jack Prouse).*

CLAY PIGEON SHOOT

An Open Clay Pigeon Shoot with Sweepstake Prizes will be held in a separate field, adjoining Car Park (commencing 11.00 a.m.— 4.00 p.m.). Guns and cartridges available on the field.

AFTERNOON PROGRAMME

CHILDREN'S RACES (Local)   PILLOW FIGHTING
1.00 p.m.   1.20 p.m.

1.45 p.m.—PARADE OF THE SOUTH DEVON FOXHOUNDS

2 p.m.—FANCY DRESS PARADE (Mounted and Unmounted)
Entry Fee at Committee Tent. 20p.
Open and Children's Classes—Prizes: 1st £1; 2nd 50p; 3rd 25p

GYMKHANA—2.15 p.m.
Entrance Fee 20p, pay at Committee Tent.
Judges: Messrs. A. Jervis and G. Wills

1—Water Carrying   6—Walk, Trot and Gallop
2—Egg & Spoon Race (under 14) 7—Musical Posts (under 14)
3—Apple Bobbing   8—Musical Posts (Open)
4—Express Letter Race   9—Wheelbarrow Race (Open)
5—Egg & Spoon Race (Open)

PRIZES IN EACH OF THE ABOVE: First £1; Second 50p; Third 25p.

3 p.m.—GRAND PARADE OF PRIZE WINNING HORSES AND PONIES, LED BY UNCLE TOM COBLEY; PRESENTATION OF CHALLENGE CUPS AND SPECIAL PRIZES AND ROSETTES.

3.45 p.m.—UNCLE TOM COBLEY NOVELTY RACE

For Perpetual Challenge Cup (presented by Keith Fox, Esq.) and prizes to the value of £12. Entrance Fee 20p. Also a Perpetual Challenge Cup (presented by the late W. F. Miners, Esq.) for first lady home. F. Nosworthy Memorial Perpetual Challenge Cup for the first Lady or Gent (Local). No competitor under 14 years allowed. Bottle of gin for first Serving man to finish. Unique Cross-country race from the top of Widecombe Hill to Show Ground.

N.B.—The Committee reserve the right to alter the time of afternoon events should it be necessary.

CONDITIONS OF ENTRY

1—Competitors who cause any delay will be disqualified. The Committee reserve the right to cancel any event.
2—No second prize unless three competitors complete the course. No third prize unless at least four complete it.
3—No competitor allowed to compete unless wearing a hard riding hat
4—All age restrictions to be counted up to and including Fair Day
Hon. Agricultural Secretary: R. P. Cruze, Pitton, Widecombe.

20

Sports and clay pigeon shoot programme. *(M. Price).*

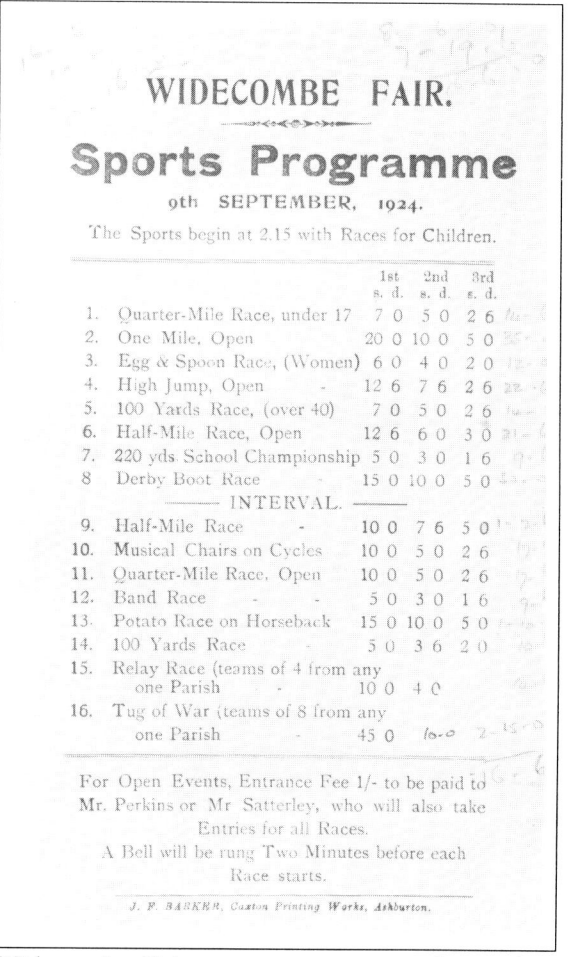

WIDECOMBE FAIR.

Sports Programme

9th SEPTEMBER, 1924.

The Sports begin at 2.15 with Races for Children.

		1st s. d.	2nd s. d.	3rd s. d.
1.	Quarter-Mile Race, under 17	7 0	5 0	2 6
2.	One Mile, Open	20 0	10 0	5 0
3.	Egg & Spoon Race, (Women)	6 0	4 0	2 0
4.	High Jump, Open	12 6	7 6	2 6
5.	100 Yards Race, (over 40)	7 0	5 0	2 6
6.	Half-Mile Race, Open	12 6	6 0	3 0
7.	220 yds. School Championship	5 0	3 0	1 6
8.	Derby Boot Race	15 0	10 0	5 0
	INTERVAL.			
9.	Half-Mile Race	10 0	7 6	5 0
10.	Musical Chairs on Cycles	10 0	5 0	2 6
11.	Quarter-Mile Race, Open	10 0	5 0	2 6
12.	Band Race	5 0	3 0	1 6
13.	Potato Race on Horseback	15 0	10 0	5 0
14.	100 Yards Race	5 0	3 6	2 0
15.	Relay Race (teams of 4 from any one Parish)	10 0	4 0	
16.	Tug of War (teams of 8 from any one Parish)	45 0		

For Open Events, Entrance Fee 1/- to be paid to Mr. Perkins or Mr Satterley, who will also take Entries for all Races.

A Bell will be rung Two Minutes before each Race starts.

J. F. BARKER, Caxton Printing Works, Ashburton.

Widecombe Fair sports programme, September 1924. *(Iris Woods).*

SPORTING LIFE AND LEISURE

Above: tug-of-war team c.1924, back row l-r: William (Bill) Langdon, Percy Prouse, William Oldrieve, Arthur Horton - front row: Thomas Nosworthy, Fred Gough, Samuel (Sam) Miners, Stanley (Stan) Norrish, William (Bill) Miners. *(Barbara Norrish)*. **Below**: tug-of-war club 1926, back row: George Nosworthy, Percy Prouse, William Satterly, Sylvester Mann, Arthur Horton, Henry Nosworthy, William Oldrieve, William Langdon - front row: Thomas Nosworthy, Fred Gough, Sam Miners, Stan Norrish, Bill Miners. *(Jack Prouse)*.

Of these photographs Sidney Beard recalled that: 'the large group would all be members of the tug-of-war club, and for each competition a team of eight would be selected, plus the coach (nine in all). It must be remembered that they were all working men and there would be some weeks when some of them would not be available due to their jobs, injury, or various other reasons, and then the team would consist of slightly different combinations. The small group would be one of these teams possibly taken at a fair, fete or similar competition. In the larger group it is the annual photo showing the trophies and cups won during the season. Sam Miners was the team coach, the one whose task was to get them all pulling together.'

WIDECOMBE

Men's morris dance team - mid 1930s; back row l-r: Sidney Harris (Jerry), Herbert Pascoe (Pickles), Jim Hine, Raymond Warren, Andrew Harvey, Cyril Daw; middle row: Wilfred Hext, Jack Prouse, Frank Dowrick, Tom Nosworthy, Sid Lang, John Chowen; front row: Ern Avery (Bungy), Ambrose Brown, Bill Bray, Alec Walters. A missing member was Henry Pascoe. *(Deborah Hannaford)*.

Women's morris dance team - mid 1930s; back row l-r: Margaret Satterly (Dowrick), Betty Brown (Colgate), Valerie Moncrieff-Brown, Mrs Withy; front row: Betty Dowrick (Walters), Margaret Nosworthy (Harris), Bessie Courtiers (Hill), Phyllis French. *(Iris Woods)*.

FOR KING AND COUNTRY

William Thorne is perhaps Widecombe's most illustrious soldier-son. The Revd Baring-Gould described him thus: 'He made his name as a wrestler, when he was induced to join the Life Guards, and in the Battle of Waterloo took part in a famous charge against the French Cuirassiers: as he was cutting down his tenth victim a shot laid him low, at the age of twenty-three.'

It appears Thorne in fact survived Waterloo as he was later decorated for the part he played there. Little else is known of his life, although the Thorne family appear in Widecombe records from 1792 up to the 1841 census when Nathaniel Thorn is recorded as living at Broadaford.

William Thorne was not the only parishioner to fight for his country. We know that two thanes at Scobitor owed loyalty to the Bishop of Coutances who was more warrior than man of god. Dynham's survey of 1566 shows that all the free tenants of Nottisworthy held their tenements and land by Knight's Service.

The names of those who fell in the two global wars of this century are recorded on the parish war memorials and elsewhere in the parish and manorial records. Those who stayed at home often joined the Home Guard, the VDF and other essential organisations and worked hard to support those who had gone away to fight the war.

A local committee also did sterling work as Jack Prouse, who served in the RAF, records: 'during the war the committee did very good work by keeping us in touch with home and sending parcels containing knitted comforts etc. all of which were greatly appreciated. They also collected substantial sums of money to make cheques possible.'

Beatrice Chase in her *Dartmoor Snapshot* series recorded the road menders at work and states on the reverse of a postcard: 'Ex-servicemen are still serving their country by road mending. The first figure is an ex-Sergeant of the 1st Devons who met Buller in the Relief of Ladysmith. The second is an ex-naval stoker who served on HMS *Ramillies* in the Great War.'

Gwen Beard tells me that the soldier was George Ford and the sailor Bill Beard. The Beatrice Chase postcard is reproduced on page 133.

Above left: Widecombe Home Guard: 'Dads' Army' (l-r): Sgt Georgie Ford, William Bennet, Taffy Davies, Edward Northmore, George Hambley, Arthur Horton, Pte Weymouth. *(Jack Prouse)*.

Above: Sgt Georgie Ford. *(Iris Woods)*.

Left: 'welcome home' card.

WIDECOMBE

TWO VILLAGE INNS

It may strike some as strange that a place as small as Widecombe should support two inns; this surely must reflect the strong community spirit, as well as the large numbers of summer visitors drawn to the village.

The Rugglestone Inn (**left**) is the smaller of the two establishments and the discreet sign is all that distinguishes it from an ordinary dwelling. It is named after a nearby logan stone - a rock of singular proportions among the many that litter the surrounding landscape. It was the original meeting place of the Friendly Society, formed in 1836. In 1801 it is known that James Lee, occupation innkeeper, lived there. The inn does not have a bar - the tap room being the living room.

The Old Inn (**left and below**) dates from the fourteenth century and has been through many alterations over the centuries. It is, like many inns, said to be haunted - by a ghost called Harry!

The top photograph (from a postcard by Chapman & Son) is postmarked 1906. Note the exterior stairway. There is a courtyard where the public bar was later built - this in turn was closed and became part of a shop.

The lower photograph (also from a postcard by Chapman & Son) was taken around 1910 and shows the inn before the public bar annexe was built. *(Ena Prowse)*.

BEATING THE BOUNDS

The parish is a centuries-old institution, set up before the Norman conquest and usually centred on the church. Boundaries defined the limits of ownership, rights and responsibilities within the parish, and created a clear delineation between one parish and its neighbours.

Prominent permanent features were chosen to mark the boundaries and these were later named and marked on maps and in parish documents.

In the years 1882-3 a Sergeant James J. Ford of the Ordnance Survey perambulated the Widecombe parish boundary and set the bounds down in a Boundary Remark Book. He was accompanied by Meresmen - local people who knew the route.

At regular intervals over the years the boundaries would be confirmed by groups of parishioners perambulating the boundary, stopping at each known mark and performing a customary action: sometimes beating the boundary mark with sticks, in other cases by bumping the youngest members of the group against the mark - presumably as a reminder for future years. This beating of the bounds is still carried out in many parishes, including Widecombe, where manor boundaries as well as the parish boundary were once regularly 'beaten'.

There were of course many disagreements, for the commoners jealously guarded their rights and even if one group were certain of their boundary, their neighbouring commoners might disagree.

It is known that at the turn of the century, when beating the manor bounds, the inhabitants of Natsworthy Manor would go through the front door of Bagpark and out through the kitchen window because the house straddled the boundary. It is likely the house was deliberately built in this way in order that common rights might be claimed in two manors.

Beating the bounds, Spitchwick Manor, 17 May 1924, (standing l-r): William Caunter, Ken Partridge, Mr Struben (Lord of the Manor), Mr West, Louis Williams, Nicholas French; (sitting l-r): Jack Cleave, Tom Cleave, Arthur Warren, Sam Cannon, Charlie French; unknown; unknown; unknown; unknown; Joe Sragg, Kimberley French (with cigarette), Jack Nosworthy, Harry Cleave (with pipe), Japser French. *(Iris Woods)*.

Beating the bounds of Dunstone Manor, 1932; l-r: Simon 'Eddie' Northmore, Bill Miners, Arthur Hern, Mr Creber, Edward Dunn, Jack Opie, Ted Sawdye, William Hern, Jim King (?), Bill Bray (boy), Ambrose Nosworthy, Olive Awdry (Lady of the Manor), H. Town, Reg Norris (boy), Col. Robert Awdry, Bill Norrish, Louis Hannaford, Joshua Horton, Harry Bray, Clifford Lamb. *(Dymond Diaries)*.

Beating the bounds of Dunstone and Blackslade Manors at Wind Tor, 1963; l-r: Tim Reep (of Chittleford), John Horton (of Tunhill), Andrew Horton, Anthony Beard (of Bittleford Parks), Raymond Warren (of Lower Dunstone), Geoffrey Michelmore (Agent), Iris Woods (of Dunstone Cottage). *(Iris Woods)*.

MY LADY OF THE MOOR

Beatrice Chase, the *nom de plume* of Olive Katharine Chase Parr, became a celebrated novelist in the early part of the present century. She was born at Harrow in Middlesex and 1874 and after working in the London slums she became very ill and eventually, with her mother, she moved to Venton were she lived for more than fifty years up to her death in 1955.

She was always an eccentric, romantically at first, but later became something of a harridan. As a young boy, the author remembers meeting her several times and by then her reputation was enough to frighten children into obedience.

Her stories and characters were imbued with romanticism: her mother, Katharine Parr, was described as 'the rainbow maker' from the coloured bead necklaces she wove; a local sheep dog was known as the 'Tweed Dog' because its coat matched the writer's skirt. 'Mr Bluejacket' was the name given to their manservant, a retired mariner, and even her typewriter was given the name 'Aquinate Remington'.

It was with her later works that she became best known - and best remembered today. *The Heart of the Moor* (1914) and *Through a Dartmoor Window* (1915), brought her national fame. John Oxenham, another local writer, made Beatrice the heroine of his book *My Lady of the Moor* and this became a title she accepted for herself.

Olive Parr was brought up in the Catholic faith and she built a small chapel at Venton, open to all, where mass was heard on a regular basis. This was the time of the Great War and Olive became involved in a number of 'good works' such as 'The Crusade for Moral Living'. She opened one of the cottages at Venton as the Little Home of Rest at St Michael's, another cottage became St Gabriel's, a third, The Anchorage.

Somewhere at the hamlet was a school but its identification is difficult due to the many rebuildings that have taken place. It was the rebuilding of the cottage alongside the '1739' longhouse which created the celebrated 'window' of her novel.

Like so many of her generation Olive lost a fiancé in the Great War, a loss from which she never recovered. After her mother's death she became more isolated and cantankerous and the final tragedy of her life was to be taken 'as a person in need of care and attention' away from her beloved moor and into hospital where she died, aged eighty.

The hamlet of Venton - home of the author Beatrice Chase.

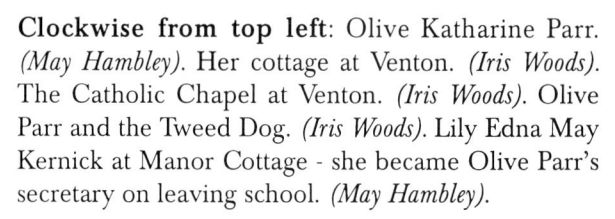

WIDECOMBE

Clockwise from top left: Olive Katharine Parr. *(May Hambley)*. Her cottage at Venton. *(Iris Woods)*. The Catholic Chapel at Venton. *(Iris Woods)*. Olive Parr and the Tweed Dog. *(Iris Woods)*. Lily Edna May Kernick at Manor Cottage - she became Olive Parr's secretary on leaving school. *(May Hambley)*.

LIST OF SUBSCRIBERS

Agar, Katherine. Harbetonford, Devon.
Allen, Elizabeth. Bexley.
Allen, Mr and Mrs K. Dousland, Devon.
Mr and Mrs G.A. Awdry. Devizes, Wilts.
John A. Baker. Exeter, Devon.
Mrs D. Basire. Lezant, Cornwall.
Mr D. Batehup. Hayward's Heath.
David Baverstock. Poundsgate, Devon.
Colin Beale. Tiverton, Devon.
A.E. Beard. Widecombe-in-the-Moor.
S.J. Beard. Widecombe-in-the-Moor.
T.P. Beard. Widecombe-in-the-Moor.
Pauline Bedborough. Exmouth, Devon.
Miss C.F. Belam. Holne, Devon.
Mrs A.M.J. Belam (née Coaker). Holne, Devon.
Fred and Phyllis Bell. Widecombe-in-the-Moor.
Rev. John H. and Dr Hazel M. Bell.
R.J.F. Bellamy. Upper Pottleton, Yorks.
Mr G. Belton. Millbrook, Torpoint.
Mr J.D. Bewsher. Paignton, Devon.
B. Bewsher. Buckfastleigh, Devon.
Alan and Susie Boult. Widecombe-in-the-Moor.
Mrs S. Boult. Widecombe-in-the-Moor.
Mrs D. Brabin. Widecombe-in-the-Moor.
G.P. Bradford. Tavistock, Devon.
S.P. Bradford. Tavistock, Devon.
Dave and Kath Brewer, Torquay, Devon.
Ashell Richard Brown. Sudbury.
Anstice Brown. Devizes, Wilts.
Mr A.J. Brown. Bovey Tracey, Devon.
Mr A Brown. Ashburton, Devon.
Revd J. and Mrs L Brown. Ashburton, Devon
Mike Brown. Plymouth, Devon.
Buckfast Abbey, Devon.
Miss L. Burge. Hatfield.
K.J. Burrow. Bucks Cross, Devon.
Marian Butler. Bovey Tracey, Devon.
Mrs M. Butler. Newton Abbot, Devon.
Anna and Simon Butler. Manaton, Devon.
Mrs E.P. Coaker. Widecombe-in-the-Moor.
Kristian Carter. Warminster, Wilts.
Richard and Valerie Casey. Widecombe-in-the-Moor.
Joyce Caunter. Paignton, Devon.
Pamela Clare. Widecombe-in-the-Moor.
Roger Cobley. Westward Ho!, Devon.
Mr H.A. Cole. Widecombe-in-the-Moor.
Dr David B. Connell. Lusleigh, Devon.
Mr and Mrs A. Cook. Plymouth, Devon.
Peter Cooper. Wadebridge, Cornwall.
Bob Cornish. Liverton, Devon.
Sylvia Coucher Needham. Widecombe-in-the-Moor.
Mrs Cruze. Widecombe-in-the-Moor.
Ann Darlington. Merriot.
Dartington Rural Archive.
Dartmoor National Park Authority.
Mrs Day. Widecombe-in-the-Moor.
Gary and Sheenagh Denham. Widecombe-in-the-Moor.
Devon and Exeter Institution.

B.S.T. Wingfield Digby. Ilsington, Devon.
John Earle. Widecombe-in-the-Moor.
Neville Enderson. Coleford, Devon.
L.A. and M.J. Ensor. Widecombe-in-the-Moor.
Richard James Farleigh. Plymouth, Devon.
Michael Ferchuck. Salcombe, Devon.
Lynne Fillery. Maidstone, Kent.
Mr Fisher. Totnes, Devon.
Miss C.F.A. Frazer. Morpeth.
Mrs B.A. French. Ponsworthy, Devon.
Michael French. Basingstoke, Hants.
Mrs M.E. Gayton. Liverton, Devon.
A.J.W. Gerrard. Harborne, Birmingham.
Michael T. Giles. Canterbury.
Mr and Mrs G.W.S. Gilliam. Tavistock, Devon.
Mrs J.V. Gooch. Widecombe-in-the-Moor.
Sheila Goodgame. Tonbridge.
A.A. Greenfield. Tavistock, Devon.
Mr and Mrs Roy Greening. Cardiff.
Elisabeth and Tom Greeves. Tavistock, Devon.
Roger Grimley. Bigbury, Devon.
Stella Grimsley. Overton, Hants.
Rina Griver. Louth.
Mrs B. Guthrie. Widecombe-in-the-Moor.
Miss K. Hall. Poundsgate, Devon.
Elizabeth J. Hambleton (née Palmer). Bovey Tracey.
Peter Hamilton-Leggett. Tavistock, Devon.
Miss D. Hannaford. Kenn, Devon.
Mr C.E. Harman. Truro, Cornwall.
Margaret and Brian Harris. Widecombe-in-the-Moor.
Bruce and Diana Harris. Ipplepen, Devon.
Mr and Mrs Harris. Okehampton, Devon.
Wilfred and Joyce Hext. Ponsworthy, Devon.
Mr D. Heyes. Tavistock, Devon.
Mr B. Hicks. Widecombe-in-the-Moor.
M.H. Hill. Ilfracombe, Devon.
Peter Hirst. Yelverton, Devon.
Tom. E. and A. Robin Hood. Torquay, Devon.
Miss G. Hooper. St Leonards.
Mrs Stella Hooton (née Brown). Harrold, Bedford.
Robert and Hazel Howard. Ystrad Neurig, Dyfed.
Miss D.J. Ide. Kingsbridge, Devon.
Miss T.B. Inglefield. Bishopsteignton, Devon.
Mr J.L. Jervoise. Sampford Courtenay, Devon.
W.R. Kernick. Liskeard, Cornwall.
Colin C. Kilvington. Stoke, Devon.
Miss Sharon Lamb. Widecombe-in-the-Moor.
Miss Audrey Lamb. Widecombe-in-the-Moor.
Mr and Mrs Lane. Tremar.
S.R. Langmead. Galmpton, Devon.
Richard Large. Widecombe-in-the-Moor.
Louie Lavis (née Hern). Bovey Tracey.
Brian Le Messurier. Exeter, Devon.
Miss J. Lee. Tavistock, Devon.
David Chown Lee. Exmouth, Devon.
H.J. Lentern. Widecombe-in-the-Moor.
J.A. Lieurance. Poundsgate, Devon.
Chris Lloyd. Henbury, Bristol.

LIST OF SUBSCRIBERS

Shirley and John Mann. Plympton, Devon.
Mr R.S. Mann. Widecombe-in-the-Moor.
Laurie Manton. Aldershot.
Douglas B. Marsh. Totnes, Devon.
Helen McCulloch, Strood.
Christopher J. McIntosh. Shanklin, Isle of Wight.
D.J. Middleweek. Widecombe-in-the-Moor.
Ted Miners. Queensland, Australia.
Andy Mitchell. Beckenham.
Peter Mold. Fremantle, Western Australia.
Terry Monckton. Portchester, Hants.
Brendan Monckton, Huntingdon.
Steve Morley. Widecombe-in-the-Moor.
Julia and Clifford Morley. Newton Abbot, Devon.
Margaret Morley (née Hannaford), Blandford Forum.
Arch & Audrey Mortimore. Widecombe-in-the-Moor.
Lloyd & Rosemary Mortimore. Widecombe-in-the-Moor.
Rodney & Jean Mortimore. Buckfastleigh.
S. and R. Mulligan. Newton Abbot, Devon.
Graham John Naylor. Plymstock, Devon.
Steve Newell. Flackwell Heath.
Mrs B.M. Norrish. Ponsworthy, Devon.
Barry J. Northcott. Boyton, Cornwall.
Misses P. and S. Nosworthy. Widecombe-in-the-Moor.
S.G. Nosworthy. Exmouth, Devon.
Mrs Dawn Nosworthy. Widecombe-in-the-Moor.
Mr M.J. Osborne. Westbury. Wilts.
Dave and Jan Ovenden. Walton on Thames.
Mr and Mrs K. Owen. Tavistock, Devon.
Mr H. Owen. Tavistock, Devon.
Mrs Phoebe Palmes. Bere Alston, Devon.
Mr and Mrs H. Pascoe. Ashburton, Devon.
Martin A. Pascoe. Cosham.
Mrs E.M. Pascoe. Widecombe-in-the-Moor.
Mr T. Pascoe. Dursley.
Mr R. Pascoe. Liverton, Devon.
Mrs Phyllis D. Pascoe. Widecombe-in-the-Moor.
Mr and Mrs M. Pascoe. Widecombe-in-the-Moor.
Mike and Jane Passmore. Exeter, Devon.
Andrew Passmore. Exeter, Devon.
L.E. and S.L. Peach. Widecombe-in-the-Moor.
Mrs M.D. Pearce. Yeovil, Somerset.
Mary Louise Pearse (née Hannaford) Tavistock, Devon.
Marion Pelham. London.
D.G. Perkins. Widecombe-in-the-Moor.
Michael Perriam. Buckland-in-the-Moor.
Mrs M.E. Phipps. Poundsgate, Devon.
Mr T. Pool. Ilsington, Devon.
Henry G. Price. Teignmouth.
Dave Privett. St Albans.
Muriel and John Prouse. Brecon.
Miss Ena M. Prowse. Ashburton, Devon.
Mr and Mrs D.W. Puttick.
Mrs V.M. Queen. Haslemere.
Mrs J.P. Reeves. Paignton, Devon.
Mr J.H. Reith, Dousland, Devon.
Paul Rendell, Plymouth, Devon.
K.J. Rickard. Lydford, Devon.

John S. Roles. Shipston-on-Stour
Mr and Mrs Rolfe. Tamerton Foliot, Devon.
Jenny Sanders. Tavistock, Devon.
Mr W.A. Saxton. Taunton, Somerset.
Mr and Mrs J. Skinner. Newton Abbot, Devon.
Mrs M. Slade. Ponsworthy, Devon.
Edward and Usha Smerdon. California, U.S.A.
J.E. Smith. Prestwich, Manchester.
Mrs Mary Stanbrook. Brixham, Devon.
Mr and Mrs F. Stanley. Kington Langley.
Robert Steemson. Postbridge, Devon.
Mary Stone. Chagford, Devon.
Leslie Sutton. Tavistock, Devon.
Anthony P. Tapp. Kelly Bray, Cornwall.
Alan Taylor. Royton, Oldham.
Mrs P. Theobald (née German). Haslemere.
Mrs L.M. Thomas. Preston, Devon.
R.C. Trembath. London.
Revd Prebendery B.R. Tubbs. Paignton, Devon.
Mrs Nel Tullis. Kenton, Devon.
C.W. Turner. Bovey Tracey, Devon.
Mrs N.K. Van Der Kiste. South Brent, Devon.
John Vickery. Poundsgate, Devon.
Dr Denys J. Voaden. Maryland, USA.
Mrs S. Walcot. Poundsgate, Devon.
Mr G. Waldron. Plymouth, Devon.
Mrs Mary Wale. Newton Abbot, Devon.
Mrs B.B.J. Wale. Southport, Merseyside.
Mr M. Warren. Widecombe-in-the-Moor.
Cllr. Ken Watson. Ashburton, Devon.
A. Watson. Exeter, Devon.
Mrs S.M. Watts. Winchester.
A.H. Way. Chickerell, Dorset.
John & Margaret Weir. Moretonhampstead, Devon.
Geoffrey Weymouth. Ponsworthy, Devon.
Mr J. Weymouth. South Brent, Devon.
Claude and Alison Whale. Widecombe-in-the-Moor.
Penny and Brian Whale.
R. Whale. Newton Abbot, Devon.
A.W. Wheelhouse. Ilsington, Devon.
Dr and Mrs E.H.T. Whitten. Widecombe-in-the-Moor.
Christopher Whittle. Bovingdon.
Freda Wilkinson. Poundsgate, Devon.
Mrs A. Williams. Poundsgate, Devon.
B.V. Williams. Paignton, Devon.
Mrs Sandra Williams. Folly Gate, Devon.
Mark Williamson. Chelmsford, Essex.
Robert R. Willis. Belstone, Devon.
Dick Wills. Ilsington, Devon.
Graham & Sandra Wooding. Widecombe-in-the-Moor.
Karen Woods. Reigate.
Andrew and Janet Woods. Portchester, Hants.
Rollo G. Woods. Swanage.
Robert Woods. Didcot.
Revd. G. Wrayford. Minehead, Somerset.
T. Wright. Newton Abbot. Devon.
Miss R. Wright. Newton Abbot, Devon.
Stephen Wrymouth. Ponsworthy, Devon.